"C. S. Lewis's narrative poem *Dymer* is indeed a 'splendour in the dark,' not only because it has been hidden in the darkness of neglect but also because, for those who read and enjoy it, there is still much that remains dark and difficult in the poetry, for all its many splendors. And here Jerry Root has done us all an immense service, by rescuing this neglected poem from obscurity and presenting us with an excellent, scholarly edition. But more than that, in the essays that follow the text, Root has shone considerable light on the poem and, through the poem, on Lewis himself."

Malcolm Guite, Girton College, Cambridge, author of *Mariner: A Theological Voyage with Samuel Taylor Coleridge*

"A delightful book that brings new life to a coming-of-age story many years in the writing, published in the 1920s by then-unbeliever C. S. Lewis, who aspired at that time to be a great poet. As a book-length poem, *Dymer* turned out to be 'a fascinating failure,' as David C. Downing deftly points out in his foreword. For Jerry Root, the main commentator on the poem, its story yields many treasures— 'splendour in the dark'—that would reappear in various genres in the future Lewis's prose, as he became an engaging writer for scholars and also wider readerships."

Colin Duriez, author of *C. S. Lewis: A Biography of Friendship* and *Dorothy L. Sayers: A Biography*

"When C. S. Lewis went to study with his tutor William T. Kirkpatrick, he delighted in the robust intellectual curriculum placed before him. It was challenging and Lewis loved it. Hard stuff. Good stuff. Nourishing for mind and soul. That is exactly the sense one gets while reading the marvelous lectures collected in this book: we are invited to study ideas of substance under the direction of a great teacher."

Diana Pavlac Glyer, professor in the Honors College at Azusa Pacific University and author of *Bandersnatch: C. S. Lewis, J. R. R. Tolkien, and the Creative Collaboration of the Inklings*

"No early work by Lewis is so foundational as his preconversion poem, *Dymer*. In excavating the ways in which Lewis's more monumental works rise from and build upon *Dymer*, Root has taken readers further down and further into that depth."

Corey Latta, author of *C. S. Lewis and the Art of Writing*

"Dr. Root masterfully brings an overlooked, preconversion piece by C. S. Lewis into the light. *Dymer* represents . . . salvation. This poem deserves serious consideration in the Lewis canon for its unique contribution in evaluating the life and work of a complex yet humane and always highly relevant spiritual thinker."

Carolyn Weber, professor and author of *Surprised by Oxford* and *Sex and the City of God*

Splendour in the Dark

C. S. LEWIS'S *DYMER* IN HIS LIFE AND WORK

JERRY ROOT

INCLUDES *DYMER: WADE ANNOTATED EDITION*
ANNOTATIONS BY DAVID C. DOWNING

Academic

An imprint of InterVarsity Press
Downers Grove, Illinois

InterVarsity Press
P.O. Box 1400, Downers Grove, IL 60515-1426
ivpress.com
email@ivpress.com

InterVarsity Press® is the book-publishing division of InterVarsity Christian Fellowship/USA®, a movement of students and faculty active on campus at hundreds of universities, colleges, and schools of nursing in the United States of America, and a member movement of the International Fellowship of Evangelical Students. For information about local and regional activities, visit intervarsity.org.

Scripture quotations, unless otherwise noted, are from The Holy Bible, English Standard Version, copyright © 2001 by Crossway Bibles, a division of Good News Publishers. Used by permission. All rights reserved.

Cover design and image composite: David Fassett
Interior design: Jeanna Wiggins
Cover image of C.S. Lewis (ca. 1918) used by permission of the Marion E. Wade Center, Wheaton College, IL.
Images: paper texture © Katsumi Murouchi / Moment Collection / Getty Images
    grunge paper texture © hudiemm / E+ / Getty Images

ISBN 978-0-8308-5375-5 (print)
ISBN 978-0-8308-5529-2 (digital)

Printed in the United States of America ∞

InterVarsity Press is committed to ecological stewardship and to the conservation of natural resources in all our operations. This book was printed using sustainably sourced paper.

Library of Congress Cataloging-in-Publication Data
A catalog record for this book is available from the Library of Congress.

P	22	21	20	19	18	17	16	15	14	13	12	11	10	9	8	7	6	5	4	3	2	1
Y	38	37	36	35	34	33	32	31	30	29	28	27	26	25	24	23	22	21	20			

TO MY BROTHER JIMMY ROOT,

WHO AS A TEACHER AND COACH

HAS INVESTED HIS LIFE IN A GENERATION

OF YOUNG MEN AND WOMEN IN SCHOOLS IN

BOTH WATTS AND PALMDALE, CALIFORNIA.

HIS LIFE IS AN INSPIRATION TO ME.

It seemed to be the low voice of the world
Brooding alone beneath the strength of things,
Murmuring of days and nights and years unfurled
Forever, and the unwearied joy that brings
Out of old fields the flowers of unborn springs,
Out of old wars and cities burned with wrong,
A splendour in the dark, a tale, a song.

DYMER, CANTO V, STANZA 29

CONTENTS

ACKNOWLEDGMENTS

I WOULD LIKE TO THANK Walter and Darlene Hansen for the privilege of delivering the Hansen lectures at the Marion E. Wade Center at Wheaton College—lectures given in honor of the memory of Ken and Jean Hansen. The very first night I ever spent in Wheaton, Illinois, in February 1980, was as a guest in Ken and Jean's home. The Hansen family has marked my life so frequently, and I am grateful. I would also like to acknowledge the late Christopher Mitchell, who first approached me about the possibility of delivering the Hansen lectures, and to thank Marjorie Lamp Mead for her encouragement to explore a fresh area of Lewis scholarship, which I found in *Dymer*. Furthermore, I am indebted to professors Jeff Davis, Mark Lewis, and Miho Nonaka for their responses after the lectures were delivered. My only regret about these presentations appearing in book form is that readers will never be able to enter into the absolute hilarity and good humor in which these responses were presented. I doubt I have ever laughed so loud in my life; it was great fun! I am also grateful to the staff at the Marion E. Wade Center at Wheaton College, without whose help these lectures and this book would never have come to the light of day: professors David and Crystal Downing, Marjorie Lamp Mead, Laura Schmidt, Mary Lynn Uitermarkt, Elaine Hooker, Aaron Hill, Shawn Mrakovich, and Hope Grant. Furthermore, I am grateful to the Rev. Dr. David McNutt of InterVarsity Press for working with me on the preparation of the manuscript for publication. Significant portions of these lectures were read and critiqued by the "Mead men": the late Lon Allison, Walter Hansen, David Henderson, and Rick Richardson. I am deeply grateful to them for their critique and feedback. I am also grateful for critical insights that have come from other close friends: Dr. Tim Tremblay, and professors Robert

Bishop, Jeff Davis, Mark Lewis, Peter Walters, and David Sveen. While studying *Dymer* I was impressed with the frequency of bird images in the text. I must acknowledge a debt therefore to Nadia Skolnitsky who opened my eyes to the significance of the *avian portent* imagery in Norse Mythology and its significance in *Dymer*. Of course, I remain constantly grateful to my wife, Claudia, for her reflections and comments on my work and to my sister, Kathy Hamlin, who first introduced me to the writings of C. S. Lewis. I am also in debt to Tim and Amy Lefever for granting me the opportunity to write and study at Bearings in Bodega Bay.

DYMER

Wade Annotated Edition

ANNOTATIONS BY
DAVID C. DOWNING

FOREWORD

David C. Downing

C. S. Lewis's first and only book-length narrative poem *Dymer* (originally published in 1926)[1] was not a literary success. But it is a fascinating failure. Published five years before Lewis's conversion to Christianity in 1931, the poem is a promising bit of apprentice work for a young writer who hadn't yet discovered which medium was best for what he wanted to say—or indeed what it was that he truly wanted to say.

In his preface to the 1950 edition of *Dymer* (later reprinted in *Narrative Poems*), Lewis explained the origins of *Dymer* and how it can best be understood:

> What I "found" what simply "came to me" was the story of a man who, on some mysterious bride, begets a monster: which monster, as soon as it has killed its father, becomes a god. This story arrived, complete, in my mind somewhere about my seventeenth year. To the best of my knowledge I did not consciously or voluntarily invent it, nor was it, in the plain sense of that word, a dream. All I know about it is that there was a time when it was not there, and then presently a time when it was. Everyone may allegorize it or psychoanalyse it as he pleases: and if I did so myself my interpretations would have no more authority than anyone else's.[2]

---

[1] Published under the pseudonym Clive Hamilton by J. M. Dent.
[2] C. S. Lewis, *Dymer: Wade Annotated Edition* in Jerry Root, *Splendour in the Dark: C. S. Lewis's Dymer in His Life and Work* (Downers Grove, IL: IVP Academic 2020), 9-10. Cf. C. S. Lewis, *Dymer* (London: J. M. Dent & Sons LTD, 1950), ix-x.

Clearly, Lewis in his early years wanted to create a "modern myth," similar to those he admired in George MacDonald and Franz Kafka. Lewis realized that most myths evolve gradually, the work of many voices over many centuries. But he believed there were also modern mythmakers, writers who could create archetypal patterns of events that transcended their actual choice of words in telling a story.

Lewis wrote a prose version of *Dymer* in 1916–1917, which has not survived. In 1918 he tried retelling the story in verse, taking his poetic form from Shakespeare's *Venus and Adonis*. In this version, the poem was called "The Redemption of Ask," after the first man named Ask, the "Adam" character in Norse mythology. Finally in 1922 Lewis recast the story in rhyme royal, a stanza form invented by Chaucer. This poetic form consists in seven-line stanzas of iambic pentameter, with end-rhymes of ABABBCC. Lewis finished the poem in 1925, and it was published by J. M. Dent in 1926.

Lewis was hoping that *Dymer* would launch his career as a poet, but it received more negative reviews than positive, and it quickly sank into oblivion. By the mid-1920s, modernist poetry was in vogue, so that traditional, metered poetry had become passé, especially narrative poems. The poem itself is uneven, beginning with overly obvious satire on planned societies, then plunging into several obscure episodes involving dream-like settings, murky characterizations, and portentous symbols. Towards the end, the poem becomes obvious again in its overt rejection of magic and occultism.

The young Lewis's power of versification was also undistinguished. Though trying to write in iambic pentameter, ten syllables per line alternating in a -/-/-/-/-/ pattern (as in Shakespeare's That TIME of YEAR thou MAYST in ME beHOLD), Lewis too often clipped his lines at nine syllables or else allowed them to run over to eleven or twelve syllables. This unevenness, along with frequent metrical irregularities, make too many lines sound like mere prose. The poem's expressive power is also undermined by the use of jarring end-rhymes (swell/unendurable; there/secreter; solitude/blood) and shopworn similes (like an ostrich hiding its head in the sand; as easy as slipping on well-worn shoes).

Even with these defects, *Dymer* played an important part in Lewis's development as a writer. Lewis was trying to write in the mythic spirit of George MacDonald. But the young Lewis shared neither MacDonald's buoyant Christian faith nor his penchant for creating stories with open-ended meanings. In his twenties, Lewis's temperament was more critical and ironic, and his writings evoked more clearly definable symbols. In places, *Dymer* verges on allegory.

Dymer may have served as a kind of self-directed sermon. In *Surprised by Joy*, Lewis recalls that, in his early years, he was living almost entirely in his imagination, and he later came to recognize that this was not a healthy condition. Thus, the figure of Dymer is almost a personification of Wishful Thinking. He assumes he can do away with authority without realizing that he is unleashing anarchy. He supposes he can just go and live in nature, ending up cold, hungry, and almost falling off a cliff. In the ghostly palace, he dreams of himself dressed as a nobleman, perhaps a leader of the people and a sought-after lover. But it is all just self-projection of the id and the ego; such narcissistic fantasies must be sacrificed if anything more powerful and beautiful is to be born.

Dymer also contains a number of motifs and images that Lewis would develop in his later works, with more vivid description and greater thematic depth. The idea of an unseen lover and a mysterious palace would appear again in the Cupid and Psyche episodes of *Till We Have Faces* (1956). The belief that individual crimes could lead to social revolution is examined again in *The Last Battle* (1956). And the suggestion that death may have the power to transform something loathsome into something beautiful is amplified in the lizard episode of *The Great Divorce* (1946).

Dymer succeeds more as a story than as a poem, a coming-of-age narrative about lost illusions and unintended consequences. At that stage of his life, Lewis seemed to understand more fully what he was against rather than what he was for. It would take another five years for Lewis to develop his own clear and compelling vision of reality and to find his voice as one of the finest prose stylists of the twentieth century.

Dedication

The first edition of *Dymer*,
published in 1926, included no
dedication. When *Dymer* was
reprinted in 1950, it was
dedicated to Marjorie Milne, a
friend of Owen Barfield's, who
introduced her to Lewis in the
1940s. A devout Roman Catholic,
she later published an essay
titled, "*Dymer*: Myth or Poem?"
(*The Month*, VIII [September
1952]: 170-73).

TO MARJORIE MILNE

Epigraph

Nine nights I hung upon the Tree,

wounded with the spear as an offering

to Odin, myself sacrificed to myself.

HÀVAMÀL

Hàvamàl: Odin's song from the Elder Eddas. This is an example of the "dying god" motif.

PREFACE TO
THE 1950 EDITION

C. S. Lewis

At its original appearance in 1926, *Dymer*, like many better books, found some good reviews and almost no readers. The idea of disturbing its repose in the grave now comes from its publishers, not from me, but I have a reason for wishing to be present at the exhumation. Nearly a quarter of a century has gone since I wrote it, and in that time things have changed both within me and round me; my old poem might be misunderstood by those who now read it for the first time.

I am told that the Persian poets draw a distinction between poetry which they have "found" and poetry which they have "brought": if you like, between the given and the invented, though they wisely refuse to identify this with the distinction between good and bad. Their terminology applies with unusual clarity to my poem. What I "found," what simply "came to me," was the story of a man who, on some mysterious bride, begets a monster: which monster, as soon as it has killed its father, becomes a god. This story arrived, complete, in my mind somewhere about my seventeenth year. To the best of my knowledge I did not consciously or voluntarily invent it, nor was it, in the plain sense of that word, a dream. All I know about it is that there was a time when it was not there, and then presently a time when it was. Every one may allegorize it or psycho-analyse it as he pleases: and if I did so myself my interpretations would have no more authority than anyone else's.

The Platonic and totalitarian state from which Dymer escapes in Canto I was a natural invention for one who detested the state in Plato's *Republic* as much as he liked everything else in Plato, and who was, by temperament, an extreme anarchist. I put into it my hatred of my old public school and my more recent hatred of the army. But I was already critical of my own anarchism. There had been a time when the sense of defiant and almost drunken liberation which fills the first two acts of *Siegfried* had completely satisfied me. Now, I thought, I knew better. My hero therefore must go through his Siegfried moment in Cantos I and II and find in Canto IV what really comes of that mood in the end. For it seemed to me that two opposite forces in man tended equally to revolt. The one criticizes and at need defies civilization because it is not good enough, the other stabs it from below and behind because it is already too good for total baseness to endure. The hero who dethrones a tyrant will therefore be first fêted and afterwards murdered by the rabble who feel a disinterested hatred of order and reason as such. Hence, in Canto IV, Bran's revolt which at once parodies and punishes Dymer's. It will be remembered that, when I wrote, the first horrors

Siegfried: The third opera in Richard Wagner's four-opera cycle, *The Ring of the Nibelung*, based on characters from the Norse sagas. In his autobiography, *Surprised by Joy*, Lewis recounts that he first learned the story of Siegfried from a written synopsis of the opera. It was not until some months later that the enraptured boy was able to listen to recordings of this heroic drama. Both Lewis and his friend J. R. R. Tolkien had a great love for Icelandic and Norse myths.

new psychology: Freudianism

Christina Pontifex: Christina Pontifex is a clergyman's wife in Samuel Butler's *The Way of All Flesh* (1903). Though outwardly modest, Christina has grandiose fantasies about her rewards in heaven: "Christina pictured herself

of the Russian Revolution were still fresh in every one's mind; and in my own country, Ulster, we had had opportunities of observing the daemonic character of popular political "causes."

In those days the <u>new psychology</u> was just beginning to make itself felt in the circles I most frequented at Oxford. This joined forces with the fact that we felt ourselves (as young men always do) to be escaping from the illusions of adolescence, and as a result we were much exercised about the problem of fantasy or wishful thinking. The "Christina Dream," as we called it (after <u>Christina Pontifex</u> in Butler's novel), was the hidden enemy whom we were all determined to unmask and defeat. My hero, therefore, had to be a man who had succumbed to its allurements and finally got the better of them. But the particular form in which this was worked out depended on two peculiarities of my own history.

(1) From at least the age of six, romantic longing— <u>Sehnsucht</u>—had played an unusually central part in my experience. Such longing is in itself the very reverse of wishful thinking: it is more like thoughtful wishing. But it throws off what may be called systems of imagery. One among many such which it had thrown off for me was the <u>Hesperian or Western Garden system</u>, mainly derived from Euripides, Milton, Morris, and the early Yeats. By the time I wrote *Dymer* I had come, under the influence of our common obsession about Christina Dreams, into a state of angry revolt against that spell. I regarded it as the very type of the illusions I was trying to escape

and Theobald [her husband] as braving the scorn of almost every other human being in the achievement of some mighty task which should redound to the honour of her Redeemer. She could face anything for this. But always toward the end of her vision there came a little coronation scene high up in the golden regions of the Heavens, and a diadem was set upon her head by the Son of Man himself, amid a host of angels and archangels who looked on in envy and admiration" (*The Way of All Flesh*, chapter 12). Later when Christina gives birth to a son, she wonders if he might become a modern-day Messiah, delivering his generation from their follies. Lewis came to believe that such flights of fancy undermined one's actual satisfactions and achievements in life.

NB: Christina was changed to "Christiana" in *Narrative Poems* (published in 1972, after Lewis's death).

Sehnsucht: A longing for the unattainable that is both an ache and a pleasure. Lewis uses his experiences of Sehnsucht (or "Joy" or "Sweet Desire") as the organizing principle in both his autobiographical allegory *The Pilgrim's Regress* (1933) and his memoir *Surprised by Joy* (1955).

Hesperian or Western Garden system: In Greek mythology, Hesperides was a western garden of trees with golden apples, guarded by a dragon. Lewis developed this imagery much more fully in *Perelandra*.

"groves and high places":
1 Kings 14:23, "For they also built them high places, and images, and groves, on every high hill, and under every green tree." The Canaanites constructed these as places for the worship of pagan deities; the Israelites wanted to destroy such centers of idolatry.

"the heresies that men leave are hated the most":
Shakespeare, *A Midsummer Night's Dream*, Act 2, scene 2.

Maeterlinck: Maurice Maeterlinck (1862–1947) was a Belgian dramatist and essayist. In his later years, he took increasing interest in spiritualism and the occult.

Yeats: William Butler Yeats (1865–1939), an Irish poet and dramatist, was one of the major figures of twentieth-century literature. By the time Lewis met him in 1921, Yeats was increasingly preoccupied with esoteric studies—Theosophy, the Kabbalah, and automatic spirit writing.

Rosa Alchemica: A romance story by Yeats with strong mystical overtones.

Voltaire, Lucretius, and Joseph McCabe: Voltaire, the pen name of Francois-Marie Arouet (1694–1778), the Enlightenment philosopher

from. It must therefore be savagely attacked. Dymer's temptation to relapse into the world of fantasy therefore comes to him (Canto VII) in that form. All through that canto I am cutting down my own former "groves and high places" and biting the hand that had fed me. I even tried to get the sneer into the metre; the archaic spelling and accentuation of *countrie* in vii. 23 is meant as parody. In all this, as I now believe, I was mistaken. Instead of repenting my idolatry I spat upon the images which only my own misunderstanding greed had ever made into idols. But "the heresies that men leave are hated most" and lovers' quarrels can be the bitterest of all.

(2) Several years before I wrote the poem, back in my teens, when my mind, except for a vigilant rejection of Christianity, had no fixed principles, and everything from strict materialism to theosophy could find by turns an entry, I had been, as boys are, temporarily attracted to what was then called "the Occult." I blundered into it innocently enough. In those days every one was reading Maeterlinck, and I wanted to improve my French. Moreover, from Yeats's early poetry it was natural to turn to his prose; and there I found to my astonishment that Yeats, unlike other romantic poets, really and literally believed in the sort of beings he put into his poems. There was no question here of "symbolism": he believed in magic. And so for a time *Rosa Alchemica* took its turn (along with Voltaire, Lucretius, and Joseph McCabe) among my serious books. You will understand that this period had ended a long time (years are longer at that age) before I set about

writing *Dymer*. By then, so far as I was anything, I was an idealist, and for an idealist all supernaturalisms were equally illusions, all "spirits" merely symbols of "Spirit" in the metaphysical sense, futile and dangerous if mistaken for facts. I put this into vii. 8. I was now quite sure that magic or spiritism of any kind was a fantasy and of all fantasies the worst. But this wholesome conviction had recently been inflamed into a violent antipathy. It had happened to me to see a man, and a man whom I loved, sink into screaming mania and finally into death under the influence, as I believed, of spiritualism. And I had also been twice admitted to the upper room in Yeats's own house in Broad Street. His conversation turned much on magic. I was overawed by his personality, and by his doctrine half fascinated and half repelled, and finally the more repelled because of the fascination.

The angel in the last canto does not of course mean that I had any Christian beliefs when I wrote the poem, any more (*si parva licet componere magnis*) than the conclusion of *Faust*, Part II, means that Goethe was a believer.

This, I think, explains all that the reader might want explained in my narrative. My hero was to be a man escaping from illusion. He begins by egregiously supposing the universe to be his friend and seems for a time to find confirmation of his belief. Then he tries, as we all try, to repeat his moment of youthful rapture. It cannot be done; the old Matriarch sees to that. On top of this rebuff comes the discovery of the consequences which his rebellion

known for his searing criticisms of the Christian Church; Lucretius (99–55 BC), the pessimistic Roman poet whom Lewis quoted in *Surprised by Joy*: "Had God designed the world, it would not be / A world so frail and faulty as we see"; Joseph McCabe (1867–1955), author of *Twelve Years in a Monastery* (1897), an account of his time as a Catholic priest before he renounced his faith.

a man whom I loved: John "Doc" Askins, the brother of Janie Moore, who dabbled in the occult, experiencing a complete mental collapse and untimely death at the age of 46. Janie Moore was the mother of Paddy Moore, a friend of Lewis's from his army service during WWI. Following Paddy's death in a battle in France in 1918, Lewis began to support Mrs. Moore and her daughter Maureen, who became his "adopted" family. Both Mrs. Moore and Maureen eventually joined Lewis and his brother Warren in their common home, The Kilns, outside Oxford.

Broad Street: Yeats's rooms in Oxford, across from Balliol College. Lewis visited Yeats there twice in March 1921.

NB: The phrase "and finally the more repelled" was omitted in *Narrative Poems* (1972).

si parva licet componere magnis: "if it be allowable to compare small things to great" from Virgil's *Eclogues*

against the City has produced. He sinks into despair and gives utterance to the pessimism which had, on the whole, been my own view about six years earlier. Hunger and a shock of real danger bring him to his senses and he at last accepts reality. But just as he is setting out on the new and soberer life, the shabbiest of all bribes is offered him; the false promise that by magic or invited illusion there may be a short cut back to the one happiness he remembers. He relapses and swallows the bait, but he has grown too mature to be really deceived. He finds that the wish-fulfillment dream leads to the fear-fulfillment dream, recovers himself, defies the Magician who had tempted him, and faces his destiny.

The physical appearance of the Magician in vi. 6-9 owes something to Yeats as I saw him. If he were now alive I would ask his pardon with shame for having repaid his hospitality by such a freedom. It was not done in malice, and the likeness is not, I think, in itself, uncomplimentary.

Since his great name here comes before us, let me take the opportunity of saluting his genius: a genius so potent that, having first revivified and transmuted that romantic tradition which he found almost on its deathbed (and invented a new kind of blank verse in the process), he could then go on to weather one of the bitterest literary revolutions we have known, embark on a second career, and, as it were with one hand, play most of the moderns off the field at their own game. If there is, as may be thought, a pride verging on insolence in his later work, such pride has never come so near to being

owes something to Yeats: Actually, the resemblance goes deeper than that. Lewis met Yeats in Oxford in March 1921 and thought that Yeats was becoming more magician than poet, given all his talk of spiritualism, the Kabbalah, and other occult topics.

excusable. It must have been difficult for him to respect either the mere Romantics who could only bewail a lost leader or the mere moderns who could see no difference between <u>*On Baile's Strand*</u> and the work of <u>Richard le Gallienne</u>.

Some may be surprised at the strength of the anti-totalitarian feeling in a poem written so long ago. I had not read <u>*Brave New World*</u> or <u>*Land Under England*</u> or <u>*The Aerodrome*</u>: nor had we yet tasted the fruits of a planned economy in our own lives. This should be a warning for critics who attempt to date ancient texts too exactly on that kind of internal evidence.

C. S. L.

On Baile's Strand: A play in verse by Yeats (1903).

Richard le Gallienne (1866–1947): A popular English poet whose works Lewis considered much inferior to those of Yeats.

Brave New World or Land Under England or The Aerodrome: All three are dystopian novels portraying totalitarian societies.

DYMER

Wade Annotated Edition

Editorial note: The following text is taken from the last edition of Dymer *published during Lewis's lifetime, the 1950 edition by J. M. Dent & Sons. Exact spelling and punctuation from this edition have been retained. For those who are interested in knowing how the 1950 reprint edition differs from the 1926 first edition, we have added a comparison chart in the Appendix. Further, in the case of textual variations between the two editions, we have included brief marginal notes indicating these differences.*

Canto: Section of a longer poem. From the Italian for "song."

CANTO I

Dymer is a nineteen-year-old man living in a totalitarian society, ironically called the Perfect City. Sitting in a dull class, he yawns and then laughs out loud. When the lecturer objects, Dymer rises and strikes him, killing the old man. Dymer leaves the city, strips off his clothes, and exults in the beauty of nature. As the sun goes down, he begins to feel cold, hungry, and lonely, sensing nature's indifference to him. Hearing ethereal music, he follows it to a clearing in the woods where he discovers a palace. Finding no one around, he goes into the open door.

CANTO I

1

Y OU stranger, long before your glance
    can light
Upon these words, time will have washed away
The moment when I first took pen to write,
With <u>all my road before me</u>—yet to-day,
Here, if at all, we meet; the unfashioned clay
Ready to both our hands; both hushed to see
That which is nowhere yet come forth and be.

Stanza 1

The poem is written in *rhyme royal*, a seven-line stanza form popularized by Chaucer. The end rhymes follow the pattern of ABABBCC.

all my road before me: Walter Hooper used these words as the title for Lewis's diary, 1922–1927, first published in 1991.

2

This moment, if you join me, we begin
A partnership where both must toil to hold
The <u>clue</u> that I caught first. We lose or win
Together; if you read, you are enrolled.
And first, a marvel—Who could
    have foretold
That in the city which men called in scorn
<u>The Perfect City</u>, Dymer could be born?

Stanza 2

clue: A thread, as the one used by Theseus to escape the labyrinth.

The Perfect City: According to Lewis's 1950 preface, this is a satire of Plato's *Republic*.

3

There you'd have thought the gods were
    smothered down
Forever, and the keys were turned on fate.
No hour was left unchartered in that town,
And love was in a schedule and the State,
Chose for <u>eugenic</u> reasons who should mate
With whom, and when. Each idle song
    and dance
Was fixed by law and nothing left to chance.

Stanza 3

eugenic: Selective breeding, sometimes including forced sterilization, to improve the species.

Stanza 4

Platonists: Followers of Plato's *Republic*, with its ideas about creating a planned and controlled society. This was the one book by Plato that Lewis disliked. He also spoke in *Surprised by Joy* about his dread of "the collective" (chapter 1).

4

For some of the last <u>Platonists</u> had founded
That city of old. And masterly they made
An island of what ought to be, surrounded
By this gross world of easier light and shade.
All answering to the master's dream they laid
The strong foundations, torturing into stone
Each bubble that the Academy had blown.

5

This people were so pure, so law-abiding,
So logical, they made the heavens afraid:
They sent the very swallows into hiding
By their appalling chastity dismayed:
More soberly the lambs in spring-time played
Because of them: and ghosts dissolved
                in shame
Before their common-sense—till Dymer came.

Stanza 6

crèche: In this context, nursery schools and child care.

6

At Dymer's birth no comets scared
                the nation,
The public <u>crèche</u> engulfed him with the rest,
And twenty separate Boards of Education
Closed round him. He was passed through
                every test,
Was vaccinated, numbered, washed
                and dressed,
Proctored, inspected, whipt,
                examined weekly,
And for some nineteen years he bore
                it meekly.

7

For nineteen years they worked upon his soul,
Refining, chipping, moulding and adorning.
Then came the moment that undid the whole—
The ripple of rude life without a warning.
It came in lecture-time one April morning
—Alas for laws and locks, reproach and praise,
Who ever learned to censor the spring days?

8

A little breeze came stirring to his cheek.
He looked up to the window. A brown bird
Perched on the sill, bent down to whet his beak
With darting head—Poor Dymer watched
    and stirred
Uneasily. The lecturer's voice he heard
Still droning from the dais. The narrow room
Was drowsy, over-solemn, filled with gloom.

Stanza 8

A brown bird: Symbol of the natural over the artificial; Romanticism over more reason-based philosophies.

9

He yawned, and a voluptuous laziness
Tingled down all his spine and loosed
    his knees,
Slow-drawn, like an invisible caress.
He laughed—The lecturer stopped like one
    that sees
A Ghost, then frowned and murmured,
    "Silence, please."
That moment saw the soul of Dymer hang
In the balance—Louder then his
    laughter rang.

Stanza 9

voluptuous: Delighting in sensual pleasure.

10

The whole room watched with
    unbelieving awe.
He rose and staggered rising. From his lips
Broke yet again the idiot-like guffaw.
He felt the spirit in his finger-tips,
Then swinging his right arm—a wide ellipse
Yet lazily—he struck the lecturer's head.
The old man tittered, lurched and dropt
    down dead.

11

Stanza 11

lark: See Percy Bysshe Shelley's "To a Skylark." With its cavorting flights and cheerful song, the lark embodies all that is naturally joyous. When the character "Lewis" in *The Great Divorce* first arrives on the outskirts of heaven, he hears a lark singing.

Out of the silent room, out of the dark
Into the sun-stream Dymer passed, and there
The sudden breezes, the high-hanging <u>lark</u>,
The milk-white clouds sailing in polished air,
Suddenly flashed about him like a blare
Of trumpets. And no cry was raised behind him,
His class sat dazed. They dared not go to
    find him.

12

Yet wonderfully some rumour spread abroad—
An inarticulate sense of life renewing
In each young heart—He whistled down
    the road:
Men said: "There's Dymer"—"Why, what's
    Dymer doing?"
"I don't know"—"Look, there's Dymer,"—
    far pursuing
With troubled eyes—A long mysterious "Oh"
Sighed from a hundred throats to see him go.

13

Down the white street and past the gate
     and forth
Beyond the wall he came to grassy places.
There was a shifting wind to West and North,
With clouds in <u>heeling</u> squadron running races.
The shadows following on the sunlight's traces
Crossed the whole field and each wild flower
     within it
With change of wavering glories
     every minute.

Stanza 13

heeling: following the wind

14

There was a river, flushed with
     rains, between
The flat fields and a forest's willowy edge.
A sauntering pace he shuffled on the green,
He kicked his boots against the crackly sedge
And tore his hands in many a <u>furzy</u> hedge.
He saw his feet and ankles gilded round
With buttercups that carpeted the ground.

Stanza 14

furzy: Covered with gorse, a spiny plant with yellow flowers, native to Ireland where Lewis grew up and elsewhere in the British Isles.

15

He looked back then. The line of a low hill
Had hid the city's towers and domes
     from sight;
He stopt: he felt a break of sunlight spill
Around him sudden waves of searching light.
Upon the earth was green, and gold, and white,
Smothering his feet. He felt his city dress
An insult to that April cheerfulness.

16

He said: "I've worn this dustheap
    long enough;
Here goes!" And forthwith in the open field
He stripped away that prison of sad stuff:
Socks, jacket, shirt and breeches off he peeled
And rose up <u>mother-naked</u> with no shield
Against the sun: then stood awhile to play
With bare toes dabbling in cold river clay.

17

Forward again, and sometimes leaping high
With arms outspread as though he
    would embrace
In one act all the circle of the sky:
Sometimes he rested in a leafier place,
And crushed the wet, cool flowers against
    his face:
And once he cried aloud, "O world, O day,
Let, let me,"—and then found no prayer to say.

18

Up furrows still unpierced with earliest crop
He marched. Through woods he strolled
    from flower to flower,
And over hills. As ointment drop by drop
Preciously meted out, so hour by hour
The day slipped through his hands: and now
    the power
Failed in his feet from walking. He was done,
Hungry and cold. That moment sank the sun.

Stanza 16

mother-naked: Naked as the day he was born. Lewis uses the same adjective to describe the character Vertue in *The Pilgrim's Regress*, just before the protagonist's baptism, his symbolic death and rebirth (Book 9, section iv).

19

He lingered—Looking up, he saw ahead
The black and bristling frontage of a wood,
And over it the large sky swimming red,
Freckled with homeward crows. Surprised
     he stood
To feel that wideness quenching his hot mood,
Then shouted, "Trembling darkness,
     trembling green,
What do you mean, wild wood, what do
     you mean?"

20

He shouted. But the solitude received
His noise into her noiselessness, his fire
Into her calm. Perhaps he half believed
Some answer yet would come to his desire.
The hushed air quivered softly like a wire
Upon his voice. It echoed, it was gone:
The quiet and the quiet dark went on.

21

He rushed into the wood. He struck
     and stumbled
On hidden roots. He groped and scratched
     his face.
The little birds woke chattering where
     he fumbled.
The stray cat stood, paw lifted, in mid-chase.
There is a windless calm in such a place:
A sense of being indoors—so crowded stand
The living trees, watching on every hand:

22

A sense of trespass—such as in the hall
Of the wrong house, one time, to me befell.
Groping between the hat-stand and
            the wall—
A clear voice from above me like a bell,
The sweet voice of a woman asking "Well?"
No more than this. And as I fled I wondered
Into whose alien story I had blundered.

23

A like thing fell to Dymer. Bending low,
Feeling his way he went. The curtained air
Sighed into sound above his head, as though
Stringed instruments and horns were
            riding there.
It passed and at its passing stirred his hair.
He stood intent to hear. He heard again
And checked his breath half-drawn, as if
            with pain.

24

That music could have crumbled
            proud belief
With doubt, or in the bosom of the sage
Madden the heart that had outmastered grief,
And flood with tears the eyes of frozen age
And turn the young man's feet to pilgrimage—
So sharp it was, so sure a path it found,
Soulward with stabbing wounds of
            bitter sound.

25

It died out on the middle of a note,
As though it failed at the urge of its
      own meaning.
It left him with life quivering at the throat,
Limbs shaken and wet cheeks and body leaning,
With strain towards the sound and
      senses gleaning
The last, least, ebbing ripple of the air,
Searching the emptied darkness,
      muttering "Where?"

26

Then followed such a time as is forgotten
With morning light, but in the passing seems
Unending. Where he grasped the branch
      was rotten,
Where he trod forth in haste the forest streams
Laid wait for him. Like men in fever dreams
Climbing an endless rope, he laboured much
And gained no ground. He reached and
      could not touch.

27

And often out of darkness like a swell
That grows up from no wind upon blue sea,
He heard the music, unendurable
In stealing sweetness wind from tree to tree.
Battered and bruised in body and soul was he
When first he saw a little lightness growing
Ahead: and from that light the sound
      was flowing.

28

The trees were fewer now: and gladly nearing
That light, he saw the stars. For sky was there,
And smoother grass, white-flowered—a
      forest clearing
Set in seven miles of forest, secreter
Than valleys in the tops of clouds, more fair
Than greenery under snow or desert water,
Or the white peace descending
      after slaughter.

29

Stanza 29

C.C.S.: Casualty Clear Station, a field hospital near the combat zone in World War I.

As some who have been wounded
      beyond healing
Wake, or half wake, once only and so bless,
Far off the lamplight travelling on the ceiling,
A disk of pale light filled with peacefulness,
And wonder if this is the C.C.S.,
Or home, or heaven, or dreams—then
      sighing win
Wise, ignorant death before the pains begin:

30

Stanza 30

Lewis acknowledged to his friend Arthur Greeves that the "empty castle theme," which begins with this stanza and following, was borrowed from George MacDonald's novel *Phantastes* (Letter from Lewis to Greeves, August 31, 1930). Though Lewis called the motif "empty castle," in *Phantastes*, MacDonald's main character actually visits an empty palace, just as Lewis's Dymer does in his poem.

So Dymer in the wood-lawn blessed the light,
A still light, rosy, clear, and filled with sound.
Here was some pile of building which the night
Made larger. Spiry shadows rose all round,
But through the open door appeared
      profound
Recesses of pure light—fire with no flame—
And out of that deep light the music came.

31

Tip-toes he slunk towards it where the grass
Was twinkling in a lane of light before
The archway. There was neither fence to pass
Nor word of challenge given, nor bolted door;
But where it's open, open evermore,
No knocker and no porter and no guard,
For very strangeness entering in grows hard.

32

Breathe not! Speak not! Walk gently.
    Someone's here.
Why have they left their house with the door
    so wide?
There must be someone. . . . Dymer hung
    in fear
Upon the threshold, longing and big-eyed.
At last he squared his shoulders, smote his side
And called, "I'm here. Now let the feast begin.
I'm coming now. I'm Dymer," and went in.

CANTO II

*Dymer walks under a great dome radiant with light
and sees himself naked in a mirror. He dresses himself
in regal apparel and eats a sumptuous feast, fanta-
sizing how he might lead the people in a revolt against
their rationalistic oppressors. He enters a low, dark
chamber filled with downy pillows and alluring fra-
grances. Dymer discovers that there is a woman in the
chamber with him, and he makes love to her.*

CANTO II

1

M ORE light. Another step, and still
        more light
Opening ahead. It swilled with soft excess
His eyes yet quivering from the dregs of night,
And it was nowhere more and nowhere less:
In it no shadows were. He could not guess
Its <u>fountain</u>. Wondering round around
        he turned:
Still on each side the level glory burned.

2

Far in the dome to where his gaze was lost
The deepening roof shone clear as stones that lie
In-shore beneath pure seas. The aisles,
        that crossed
Like forests of white stone their arms on high,
Past pillar after pillar dragged his eye
In unobscured perspective, till the sight
Was weary. And there also was the light.

3

Look with my eyes. Conceive yourself above
And hanging in the dome: and thence
        through space
Look down. See Dymer, dwarfed and naked, move,
A white blot on the floor, at such a pace
As boats that hardly seem to have changed place
Once in an hour when from the cliffs we spy
The same ship always smoking towards the sky.

4

The shouting mood had withered from
    his heart;
The oppression of huge places wrapped
    him round.
A great misgiving sent its fluttering dart
Deep into him—some fear of being found,
Some hope to find he knew not what.
    The sound
Of music, never ceasing, took the rôle
Of silence and like silence numbed his soul.

Stanza 4

The oppression of huge places: Ransom has a similar experience of feeling daunted by the seemingly infinite sea and sky in *Perelandra* (chapter 13).

5

Till, as he turned a corner, his deep awe
Broke with a sudden start. For straight ahead,
Far off, a wild-eyed, naked man he saw
That came to meet him: and beyond was spread
Yet further depth of light. With quickening
    tread
He leaped towards the shape. Then stopped
    and smiled
Before a mirror, wondering like a child.

6

Beside the glass, unguarded, for the claiming,
Like a great patch of flowers upon the wall
Hung every kind of clothes: silk,
    feathers flaming,
Leopard skin, furry mantles like the fall
Of deep mid-winter snows. Upon them all
Hung the faint smell of cedar, and the dyes
Were bright as blood and clear as morning skies.

7

He turned from the white spectre in the glass
And looked at these. Remember, he had worn
Thro' winter slush, thro' summer flowers
    and grass
One kind of solemn stuff since he was born,
With badge of year and rank. He laughed
    in scorn
And cried, "Here is no law, nor eye to see,
Nor leave of entry given. Why should there be?

8

"Have done with that—you threw it
    all behind.
Henceforth I ask no licence where I need.
It's on, on, on, though I go mad and blind,
Though knees ache and lungs labour and
    feet bleed,
Or else—it's home again: to sleep and feed,
And work, and hate them always and obey
And loathe the punctual rise of each new day."

9

He made mad work among them as
    he dressed,
With motley choice and litter on the floor,
And each thing as he found it seemed the best.
He wondered that he had not known before
How fair a man he was. "I'll creep no more
In secret," Dymer said. "But I'll go back
And drive them all to freedom on this track."

Stanza 9

motley: an odd assortment

10

He turned towards the glass. The space
    looked smaller
Behind him now. Himself in royal guise
Filled the whole frame—a nobler shape
    and taller,
Till suddenly he started with surprise,
Catching, by chance, his own familiar eyes,
Fevered, yet still the same, without their share
Of bravery, undeceived and watching there.

11

Yet, as he turned, he cried, "The rest remain. . . .
If they rebelled . . . if they should find me here,
We'd pluck the whole taut fabric from
    the strain,
Hew down the city, let live earth appear!
—Old men and barren women whom
    through fear
We have suffered to be masters in our home,
Hide! hide! for we are angry and we come."

12

Thus feeding on vain fancy, covering round
His hunger, his great loneliness arraying
In facile dreams until the qualm was drowned,
The boy went on. Through endless
    arches straying
With casual tread he sauntered,
    manly playing
At manhood lest more loss of faith betide him,
Till lo! he saw a table set beside him.

Stanza 12

boy: Lewis had an unhappy boyhood in English boarding schools, and he nearly always uses the word *boy* to suggest callowness, noisiness, a loss of simplicity and wonder.

13

When Dymer saw this sight, he leaped
    for mirth,
He clapped his hands, his eye lit like a lover's.
He had a hunger in him that was worth
Ten cities. Here was silver, glass and covers.
Cold peacock, prawns in aspic, eggs
    of <u>plovers</u>,
Raised pies that stood like castles,
    gleaming fishes
And bright fruit with broad leaves around
    the dishes.

14

If ever you have passed a café door
And lingered in the dusk of a June day,
Fresh from the road, sweat-sodden and
    foot-sore,
And heard the plates clink and the music play,
With laughter, with white tables far away,
With many lights—conceive how Dymer ran
To table, looked once round him, and began.

15

That table seemed unending. Here and there
Were broken meats, bread crumbled,
    flowers defaced
—A napkin, with white petals, on a chair,
—A glass already tasted, still to taste.
It seemed that a great host had fed in haste
And gone: yet left a thousand places more
Untouched, wherein no guest had sat before.

16

There in the lonely splendour Dymer ate,
As thieves eat, ever watching, half in fear.
He blamed his evil fortune. "I come late.
Whose <u>board</u> was this? What company
    sat here?
What women with wise mouths, what
    comrades dear
Who would have made me welcome as the one
Free-born of all my race and cried, Well done!"

17

Remember, yet again, he had grown up
On <u>rations</u> and on scientific food,
At common boards, with water in his cup,
One <u>mess</u> alike for every day and mood:
But here, at his right hand, a <u>flagon</u> stood.
He raised it, paused before he drank,
    and laughed.
"I'll drown their Perfect City in this draught."

18

He fingered the cold neck. He saw within,
Like a strange sky, some liquor that
    foamed blue
And murmured. Standing now with
    pointed chin
And head thrown back, he tasted. Rapture flew
Through every vein. That moment
    louder grew
The music and swelled forth a trumpet note.
He ceased and put one hand up to his throat.

Stanza 16

board: table for serving meals

Stanza 17

rations, mess: These terms suggest bland, unvaried army meals, such as those Lewis experienced during his military service in World War I.

flagon: a drinking vessel with a handle and lid; tankard

19

Then heedlessly he let the flagon sink
In his right hand. His staring eyes were caught
In distance, as of one who tries to think
A thought that is still waiting to be thought.
There was a riot in his heart that brought
The loud blood to the temples. A great voice
Sprang to his lips unsummoned, with
         no choice.

20

"Ah! but the eyes are open, the dream
         is broken!
To sack the Perfect City? . . . a fool's deed
For Dymer! Folly of follies I have spoken!
I am the wanderer, new born, newly freed. . . .
A thousand times they have warned me of
         men's greed
For joy, for the good that all desire, but never
Till now I knew the wild heat of the endeavour.

21

"Some day I will come back to break the City,
—Not now. Perhaps when age is white
         and bleak
—Not now. I am in haste. O God, the pity
Of all my life till this, groping and weak,
The shadow of itself! But now to seek
That true most ancient glory whose
         white glance
Was lost through the whole world by
         evil chance!

22

"I was a dull, cowed thing from the beginning.
Dymer the drudge, the <u>blackleg</u> who obeyed.
Desire shall teach me now. If this be sinning,
Good luck to it! O splendour long delayed,
Beautiful world of mine, O world arrayed
For bridal, flower and forest, wave and field,
I come to be your lover. Loveliest, yield!

Stanza 22

blackleg: In Britain, a worker
who defies the unions; a *scab* in
American slang.

23

"World, I will prove you. Lest it should be said
There was a man who loved the earth: his heart
Was nothing but that love. With doting tread
He worship the loved grass: and every start
Of every bird from cover, the least part
Of every flower he held in awe. Yet earth
Gave him no joy between his death and birth.

24

"I know my good is hidden at your breast.
There is a sound of great good in my ear,
Like wings. And, oh! this moment is the best;
I shall not fail—I taste it—it comes near.
As men from a dark dungeon see the clear
Stars shining and the filled streams far away,
I hear your promise booming and obey.

25

"This forest lies a thousand miles, perhaps,
Beyond where I am come. And farther still
The rivers wander seaward with smooth lapse,
And there is cliff and cottage, tower and hill.

Somewhere, before the world's end, I shall fill
My spirit at earth's pap. For earth must hold
One rich thing sealed as Dymer's from of old.

26

"One rich thing—or, it may be, more
          than this. . . .
Might I not reach the borders of a land
That ought to have been mine? And there,
          the bliss
Of free speech, there the eyes that understand,
The men free grown, not modelled by the hand
Of masters—men that know, or men that seek,
—They will not gape and murmur when I speak."

27

Then, as he ceased, amid the farther wall
He saw a curtained and low lintelled door;
—Dark curtains, sweepy fold, night-purple pall,
He thought he had not noticed it before.
Sudden desire for darkness overbore
His will, and drew him towards it. All was blind
Within. He passed. The curtains closed behind.

28

He entered in a void. Night-scented flowers
Breathed there, but this was darker than
          the night
That is most black with beating
          thunder-showers,
—A disembodied world where depth and height
And distance were unmade. No seam of light

Showed through. It was a world not made
    for seeing,
One pure, one undivided sense of being.

29

Through darkness smooth as amber,
    warily, slowly
He moved. The floor was soft beneath his feet.
A cool smell that was holy and unholy,
Sharp like the very spring and roughly sweet,
Blew towards him: and he felt his fingers meet
Broad leaves and wiry stems that at his will
Unclosed before and closed behind him still.

30

With body intent he felt the foliage quiver
On breast and thighs. With groping arms
    he made
Wide passes in the air. A sacred shiver
Of joy from the heart's centre oddly strayed
To every nerve. Deep sighing, much afraid,
Much wondering, he went on: then,
    stooping, found
A knee-depth of warm pillows on the ground.

31

And there it was sweet rapture to lie still,
Eyes open on the dark. A flowing health
Bathed him from head to foot and great goodwill
Rose springing in his heart and poured
    its wealth
Outwards. Then came a hand as if by stealth

Out of the dark and touched his hand:
    and after
The beating silence budded into laughter:

32

—A low grave laugh and rounded like a pearl,
Mysterious, filled with home. He
    opened wide
His arms. The breathing body of a girl
Slid into them. From the world's end,
    with the stride
Of <u>seven-league boots</u> came passion to
    his side.
Then, meeting mouths, soft-falling hair, a cry,
Heart-shaken flank, sudden cool-folded
    thigh:

33

The same night swelled the mushroom in
    earth's lap
And silvered the wet fields: it drew the bud
From hiding and led on the rhythmic sap
And sent the young wolves thirsting
    after blood,
And, wheeling the big seas, made ebb
    and flood
Along the shores of earth: and held these two
In dead sleep till the time of morning dew.

Stanza 32

seven-league boots: A league is about three miles, so seven-league boots have a giant's stride of twenty-one miles. Hence, moving rapidly. NB: "Seven-league" was changed to "seven-leagued" in *Narrative Poems* (1972).

CANTO III

Dymer awakens and goes out to enjoy the dewy
freshness of the woods around him, filled with birds
and bright flowers. But when he goes back to the
palace, he is not sure if he has found the right way. His
mysterious lover seems to be gone, and a hideous old
crone bars his way back inside. Dymer tries to force
his way past her, but he is injured in the struggle and
flees back into the woods.

CANTO III

1

H E woke, and all at once before his eyes
    The pale spires of the chestnut-trees
        in bloom
Rose waving and, beyond, dove-coloured skies;
But where he lay was dark and, out of gloom,
He saw them, through the doorway of a room
Full of strange scents and softness,
        padded deep
With growing leaves, heavy with last
        night's sleep.

2

He rubbed his eyes. He felt that
        chamber wreathing
New sleepiness around him. At his side
He was aware of warmth and quiet breathing.
Twice he sank back, loose-limbed and
        drowsy-eyed;
But the wind came even there. A sparrow cried

And the wood shone without. Then
     Dymer rose,
—"Just for one glance," he said, and went,
     tip-toes,

3

Stanza 3

wagtail: A small bird like a
finch with a bobbing tail.

Out into crisp grey air and drenching grass.
The whitened cobweb sparkling in its place
Clung to his feet. He saw the <u>wagtail</u> pass
Beside him and the thrush: and from his face
Felt the thin-scented winds divinely chase
The flush of sleep. Far off he saw, between
The trees, long morning shadows of dark green.

4

Stanza 4

NB: "wheeling" was changed to
"wheeled" in *Narrative Poems*
(1972).

He stretched his lazy arms to their full height,
Yawning, and sighed and laughed, and
     sighed anew;
Then wandered farther, watching with delight
How his broad naked footprints stained the dew,
—Pressing his foot to feel the cold come through
Between the spreading toes—then
     wheeling round
Each moment to some new, shrill forest sound.

5

The wood with its cold flowers had
     nothing there
More beautiful than he, new waked from sleep,
New born from joy. His soul lay very bare
That moment to life's touch, and
     pondering deep

Now first he knew that no desire could keep
These hours for always, and that men do die
—But oh, the present glory of lungs and eye!

6

He thought: "At home they are waking now.
    The stair
Is filled with feet. The bells clang—far from me.
Where am I now? I could not point to where
The City lies from here," . . . then, suddenly,
"If I were here alone, these woods could be
A frightful place! But now I have met my friend
Who loves me, we can talk to the road's end."

7

Thus, quickening with the sweetness of the tale
Of his new love, he turned. He saw, between
The young leaves, where the palace walls
    showed pale
With chilly stone: but far above the green,
Springing like cliffs in air, the towers were seen,
Making more quiet yet the quiet dawn.
Thither he came. He reached the open lawn.

8

No bird was moving here. Against the wall
Out of the unscythed grass the nettle grew.
The doors stood open wide, but no footfall
Rang in the colonnades. Whispering through
Arches and hollow halls the light wind blew. . . .
His awe returned. He whistled—then, no more,
It's better to plunge in by the first door.

9

But then the vastness threw him into doubt.
Was this the door that he had found last night?
Or that, beneath the tower? Had he come out
This side at all? As the first snow falls light
With following rain before the year grows white,
So the first, dim foreboding touched his mind,
Gently as yet, and easily thrust behind.

10

And with it came the thought, "I do not know
Her name—no, nor her face." But still his mood
Ran blithely as he felt the morning blow
About him, and the earth-smell in the wood
Seemed waking for long hours that must
          be good
Here, in the unfettered lands, that knew
          no cause
For grudging—out of reach of the old laws.

11

He hastened to one entry. Up the stair,
Beneath the pillared porch, without delay,
He ran—then halted suddenly: for there
Across the quiet threshold something lay,
A bundle, a dark mass that barred the way.
He looked again, and lo, the formless pile
Under his eyes was moving all the while.

12

And it had hands, pale hands of wrinkled flesh,
Puckered and gnarled with vast antiquity,

That moved. He eyed the sprawling thing afresh,
And bit by bit (so faces come to be
In the red coal) yet surely, he could see
That the swathed hugeness was
    uncleanly human,
A living thing, the likeness of a woman.

13

In the centre a draped <u>hummock</u> marked
    the head;
Thence flowed the broader lines with curve
    and fold
Spreading as oak roots do. You would have said
A man could hide among them and grow old
In finding a way out. Breasts manifold
As of the <u>Ephesian Artemis</u> might be
Under that robe. The face he did not see.

Stanza 13

hummock: In this context, a hump.

NB: "Breasts" was changed to "Breast" (singular) in *Narrative Poems* (1972).

Ephesian Artemis: a Middle Eastern fertility goddess

14

And all his being answered, "Not that way!"
Never a word he spoke. Stealthily creeping
Back from the door he drew. Quick! No delay!
Quick, quick, but very quiet!—backward
    peeping
Till fairly out of sight. Then shouting, leaping,
Shaking himself, he ran—as puppies do
From bathing—till that door was out of view.

15

Another gate—and empty. In he went
And found a courtyard open to the sky,
Amidst it dripped a fountain. Heavy scent

Of flowers was here; the foxglove standing high
Sheltered the whining wasp. With hasty eye
He travelled round the walls. One doorway led
Within: one showed a further court ahead.

16

He ran up to the first—a hungry lover,
And not yet taught to endure, not blunted yet,
But weary of long waiting to discover
That loved one's face. Before his foot was set
On the first stair, he felt the sudden sweat
Cold on his sides. That sprawling mass in view,
That shape—the horror of heaviness—here too.

17

He fell back from the porch. Not yet—not yet—
There must be other ways where he would meet
No watcher in the door. He would not let
The fear rise, nor hope falter, nor defeat
Be entered in his thoughts. A sultry heat
Seemed to have filled the day. His breath
          came short,
And he passed on into that inner court.

18

And (like a dream) the sight he feared to find
Was waiting here. Then cloister, path
          and square
He hastened through: down paths that
          ended blind,
Traced and retraced his steps. The thing
          sat there

In every door, still watching, everywhere,
Behind, ahead, all round—So! Steady now,
Lest panic comes. He stopped. He wiped
    his brow.

19

But, as he strove to rally, came the thought
That he had dreamed of such a place before
—Knew how it all would end. He must
    be caught
Early or late. No good! But all the more
He raged with passionate will that overbore
That knowledge: and cried out, and beat
    his head,
Raving, upon the senseless walls, and said:

20

"Where? Where? Dear, look once out. Give
    but one sign.
It's I, I, Dymer. Are you chained and hidden?
What have they done to her? Loose her! She
    is mine.
Through stone and iron, haunted and
    hag-ridden,
I'll come to you—no stranger, nor unbidden,
It's I. Don't fear them. Shout above them all.
Can you not hear? I'll follow at your call."

21

From every arch the echo of his cry
Returned. Then all was silent, and he knew
There was no other way. He must pass by

That horror: tread her down, force his
    way through,
Or die upon the threshold. And this too
Had all been in a dream. He felt his heart
Beating as if his throat would burst apart.

22

There was no other way. He stood a space
And pondered it. Then, gathering up his will,
He went to the next door. The pillared place
Beneath the porch was dark. The air was still,
Moss on the steps. He felt her presence fill
The threshold with dull life. Here too was she.
This time he raised his eyes and dared to see.

23

Pah! Only an old woman! . . . but the size,
The old, old matriarchal dreadfulness,
Immovable, intolerable . . . the eyes
Hidden, the hidden head, the winding dress,
Corpselike. . . . The weight of the brute that
    seemed to press
Upon his heart and breathing. Then he heard
His own voice, strange and humbled, take
    the word.

24

"Good Mother, let me pass. I have a friend
To look for in this house. I slept the night
And feasted here—it was my journey's end,
—I found it by the music and the light,
And no one kept the doors, and I did right

To enter—did I not? Now, Mother, pray,
Let me pass in . . . good Mother, give me way."

25

The woman answered nothing: but he saw
The hands, like crabs, still wandering on her knee.
"Mother, if I have broken any law,
I'll ask a pardon once: then let it be,
—Once is enough—and leave the passage free.
I am in haste. And though it were a sin
By all the laws you have, I must go in."

26

Courage was rising in him now. He said,
"Out of my path, old woman. For this cause
I am new born, new freed, and here new wed,
That I might be the breaker of bad laws.
The frost of old forbiddings breaks and thaws
Wherever my feet fall. I bring to birth
Under its crust the green, ungrudging earth."

27

He had started, bowing low: but now he stood
Stretched to his height. His own voice in
    his breast
Made misery pompous, firing all his blood.
"Enough," he cried. "Give place. You shall
    not wrest
My love from me. I journey on a quest
You cannot understand, whose strength
    shall bear me
Through fire and earth. A bogy will not scare me.

28

"I am the sword of spring; I am the truth.
Old night, put out your stars, the dawn is here,
The sleeper's wakening, and the wings
          of youth.
With crumbling veneration and cowed fear
I make no truce. My loved one, live and dear,
Waits for me. Let me in! I fled the City,
Shall I fear you or . . . Mother, ah, for pity."

29

For his high mood fell shattered. Like a man
Unnerved, in bayonet-fighting, in the thick,
—Full of red rum and cheers when he began,
Now, in a dream, muttering: "I've not the trick.
It's no good. I'm no good. They're all too quick.
There! Look there! Look at that!"—so
          Dymer stood,
Suddenly drained of hope. It was no good.

30

He pleaded then. Shame beneath shame.
          "Forgive.
It may be there are powers I cannot break.
If you are of them, speak. Speak. Let me live.
I ask so small a thing. I beg. I make
My body a living prayer whose force
          would shake
The mountains. I'll recant—confess my sin—
But this once let me pass. I must go in."

31

"Yield but one inch, once only from your law;
Set any price—I will give all, obey
All else but this, hold your least word in awe,
Give you no cause for anger from this day.
Answer! The least things living when they pray
As I pray now bear witness. They speak true
Against God. Answer! Mother, let
     me through."

32

Then when he heard no answer, mad with fear
And with desire, too strained with both
     to know
What he desired or feared, yet staggering near,
He forced himself towards her and bent low
For grappling. Then came darkness.
     Then a blow
Fell on his heart, he thought. There came
     a blank
Of all things. As the dead sink, down he sank.

33

The first big drops are rattling on the trees,
The sky is copper dark, low thunder pealing.
See Dymer with drooped head and
     knocking knees
Comes from the porch. Then slowly,
     drunkly reeling,
Blind, beaten, broken, past desire of healing,
Past knowledge of his misery, he goes on
Under the first dark trees and now is gone.

CANTO IV

*Dymer is caught in the open during a fierce thunder-
storm, despairing that he never actually saw his lover
or learned her name. He meets a mortally wounded
man, who tells him that Dymer's act of violence
against his teacher spawned a revolution led by a
hunchback named Bran. The mob violence quickly
spread, and the revolutionaries began calling each
other traitors or reactionaries. The man's hands and
feet were cut off, and he was left to die. Not realizing
who he is talking to, the mutilated man curses Dymer
and wishes he could kill him.*

CANTO IV

1

FIRST came the peal that split the
                  heavens apart
Straight overhead. Then silence. Then the rain;
Twelve miles of downward water like one dart,
And in one leap were launched along the plain,
To break the budding flower and flood the grain,
And keep with dripping sound an undersong
Amid the wheeling thunder all night long.

2

Stanza 2

tattoo: rapid tapping, as on a
drum

He put his hands before his face. He stooped,
Blind with his hair. The loud drops'
                  grim tattoo
Beat him to earth. Like summer grass
                  he drooped,
Amazed, while sheeted lightning large and blue

Blinked wide and pricked the quivering
    eyeball through.
Then, scrambling to his feet, with downward head
He fought into the tempest as chance led.

3

The wood was mad. <u>Soughing</u> of branch
    and straining
Was there: drumming of water. Light was none,
Nor knowledge of himself. The trees'
    complaining
And his own throbbing heart seemed mixed
    in one,
One sense of bitter loss and beauty undone;
All else was blur and chaos and rain-steam
And noise and the confusion of a dream.

Stanza 3

Soughing: sighing, moaning

NB: "rain-steam" was changed to "rain-stream" in *Narrative Poems* (1972).

4

Aha! . . . Earth hates a miserable man:
Against him even the clouds and winds conspire.
Heaven's voice smote Dymer's ear-drum as
    he ran,
Its red throat plagued the dark with corded fire
—Barbed flame, coiled flame that ran like
    living wire
Charged with disastrous current, left and right
About his path, hell-blue or staring white.

5

Stab! Stab! Blast all at once. What's he to fear?
Look there—that cedar shrivelling in
    swift blight

Even where he stood! And there—ah, that
        came near!
Oh, if some shaft would break his soul outright,
What ease so to unload and scatter quite
On the darkness this wild beating in his skull,
Too burning to endure, too tense and full.

6

All lost: and driven away: even her name
Unknown. O fool, to have wasted for a kiss
Time when they could have talked! An
        angry shame
Was in him. He had worshipt earth, and this
—The venomed clouds fire spitting from
        the abyss,
This was the truth indeed, the world's intent
Unmasked and naked now, the thing it meant.

7

The storm lay on the forest a great time
—Wheeled in its thundery circuit,
        turned, returned.
Still through the dead-leaved darkness,
        through the slime
Of standing pools and slots of clay
        storm-churned
Went Dymer. Still the knotty
        lightning burned
Along black air. He heard the
        unbroken sound
Of water rising in the hollower ground.

8

He cursed it in his madness, flung it back,
Sorrow as wild as young men's sorrows are,
Till, after midnight, when the tempest's track
Drew off, between two clouds appeared one star.
Then his mood changed. And this was
    heavier far,
When bit by bit, rarer and still more rare,
The weakening thunder ceased from the
    cleansed air;

9

When leaves began to drip with dying rain
And trees showed black against the
    glimmering sky,
When the night-birds flapped out and
    called again
Above him: when the silence cool and shy
Came stealing to its own, and streams ran by
Now audible amid the rustling wood
—Oh, then came the worst hour for flesh
    and blood.

10

It was no nightmare now with fiery stream
Too horrible to last, able to blend
Itself and all things in one hurrying dream;
It was the waking world that will not end
Because hearts break, that is not foe
    nor friend,
Where sane and settled knowledge first appears
Of work-day desolation, with no tears.

11

He halted then, footsore, weary to death,
And heard his heart beating in solitude,
When suddenly the sound of sharpest breath
Indrawn with pain and the raw smell of blood
Surprised his sense. Near by to where he stood
Came a long whimpering moan—a
         broken word,
A rustle of leaves where some live body stirred.

12

He groped towards the sound. "What,
         brother, brother,
Who groaned?"—"I'm hit. I'm finished.
         Let me be."
—"Put out your hand, then. Reach me. No,
         the other."
—"Don't touch. Fool! Damn you! Leave
         me."—"I can't see.
Where are you?" Then more groans. "They've
         done for me.
I've no hands. Don't come near me. No, but stay,
Don't leave me . . . O my God! Is it near day?"

13

—"Soon now, a little longer. Can you sleep?
I'll watch for you."—"Sleep, is it? That's ahead,
But none till then. Listen: I've bled too deep
To last out till the morning. I'll be dead
Within the hour—sleep then. I've heard it said
They don't mind at the last, but this is Hell.
If I'd the strength—I have such things to tell."

14

All trembling in the dark and sweated over
Like a man reared in peace, unused to pain,
Sat Dymer near him in the lightless cover,
Afraid to touch and shamefaced to refrain.
Then bit by bit and often checked again
With agony the voice told on. (The place
Was dark, that neither saw the other's face.)

15

"There is a City which men call in scorn
The Perfect City—eastward of this wood—
You've heard about the place. There I was born.
I'm one of them, their work. Their sober mood,
The ordered life, the laws, are in my blood
—A life . . . well, less than happy, something more
Than the red greed and lusts that went before.

16

"All in one day, one man and at one blow
Brought ruin on us all. There was a boy
—Blue eyes, large limbs, were all he had to show,
You need no greater prophets to destroy.
He seemed a man asleep. Sorrow and joy
Had passed him by—the dreamiest, safest man,
The most obscure, until this curse began.

17

"Then—how or why it was, I cannot say—
This Dymer, this fool baby pink-and-white,
Went mad beneath his quiet face. One day,
With nothing said, he rose and laughed outright

Before his master: then, in all our sight,
Even where we sat to watch, he struck him dead
And screamed with laughter once again and fled.

18

"Lord! how it all comes back. How still the
    place is,
And he there lying dead . . . only the sound
Of a <u>bluebottle</u> buzzing . . . sharpened faces
Strained, gaping from the benches all around . . .
The dead man hunched and quiet with
    no wound,
And minute after minute terror creeping
With dreadful hopes to set the wild
    heart leaping.

19

"Then one by one at random (no word spoken)
We slipt out to the sunlight and away.
We felt the empty sense of something broken
And comfortless adventure all that day.
Men loitered at their work and could not say
What trembled at their lips or what new light
Was in girls' eyes. Yet we endured till night.

20

"Then . . . I was lying wide awake in bed,
Shot through with tremulous thought, lame
    hopes, and sweet
Desire of reckless days—with burning head.
And then there came a clamour from the street,
Came nearer, nearer, nearer—stamping feet

And screaming song and curses and a shout
Of 'Who's for Dymer, Dymer?—Up and out!'

21
"We looked out from our window.
    Thronging there
A thousand of our people, girls and men,
Raved and reviled and shouted by the glare
Of torches and of bonfire blaze. And then
Came tumult from the street beyond: again
'Dymer!' they cried. And farther off there came
The sound of gun-fire and the gleam of flame.

22
"I rushed down with the rest. Oh, we were mad!
After this, it's all nightmare. The black sky
Between the housetops framed was all we had
To tell us that the old world could not die
And that we were no gods. The flood ran high
When first I came, but after was the worse,
Oh, to recall . . . ! On Dymer rest the curse!

23
"Our leader was a hunchback with red hair
—Bran was his name. He had that kind of force
About him that will hold your eyes fast there
As in ten miles of green one patch of gorse
Will hold them—do you know? His lips
    were coarse,
But his eyes like a prophet's—seemed to fill
The whole face. And his tongue was
    never still.

24

"He cried: 'As Dymer broke, we'll break
    the chain.
The world is free. They taught you to be chaste
And labour and bear orders and refrain.
Refrain? From what? All's good enough.
    We'll taste
Whatever is. Life murmurs from the waste
Beneath the mind . . . who made the
    reasoning part
The jailer of the wild gods in the heart?'

25

"We were a ragtail crew—wild-haired,
    half-dressed,
All shouting, 'Up, for Dymer! Up away!'
Yet each one always watching all the rest
And looking to his back. And some were gay
Like drunk men, some were cringing,
    pinched and grey
With terror dry on the lip. (The older ones
Had had the sense enough to bring their guns.)

26

Stanza 26

In his 1950 preface, Lewis notes that this section depicting a mob in revolt was suggested by the Russian Revolution as well as ongoing unrest in his native Ireland.

"The wave where I was swallowed swelled
    and broke,
After long surge, into the open square.
And here there was more light: new
    clamour woke.
Here first I heard the bullets sting the air
And went hot round the heart. Our lords
    were there

In barricade with all their loyal men.
For every one man loyal Bran led ten.

27

"Then charge and cheer and bubbling sobs
    of death,
We hovered on their front. Like swarming bees
Their spraying bullets came—no time for breath.
<u>I saw men's stomachs</u> fall out on their knees;
And shouting faces, while they shouted, freeze
Into black, bony masks. Before we knew
We're into them. . . . 'Swine!'—'Die, then!'—
    'That's for you!'

Stanza 27

I saw men's stomachs: Lewis witnessed similar horrific scenes during his time in the trenches of World War I.

28

"The next that I remember was a lull
And <u>sated</u> pause. I saw an old, old man
Lying before my feet with shattered skull,
And both my arms dripped red. And then
    came Bran
And at his heels a hundred murderers ran,
With prisoners now, clamouring to take and
    try them
And burn them, wedge their nails up,
    crucify them.

Stanza 28

sated: Satisfied or even overly full.

29

"God! . . . Once the lying spirit of a cause
With maddening words dethrones the mind
    of men,
They're past the reach of prayer. The eternal laws
Hate them. Their eyes will not come clean again,

But doom and strong delusion drive them then
Without ruth, without rest . . . the iron laughter
Of the immortal mouths goes hooting after.

30
"And we had firebrands too. Tower after tower
Fell sheathed in thundering flame. The street
                    was like
A furnace mouth. We had them in our power!
Then was the time to mock them and to strike,
To flay men and spit women on the pike,
Bidding them dance. Wherever the most shame
Was done the doer called on Dymer's name.

31
"Faces of men in torture . . . from my mind
They will not go away. The East lay still
In darkness when we left the town behind
Flaming to light the fields. We'd had our will:
We sang, 'Oh, we will make the frost distil
From Time's grey forehead into living dew
And break whatever has been and build new.'

32
"Day found us on the border of this wood,
Blear-eyed and pale. Then the most part began
To murmur and to lag, crying for food
And shelter. But we dared not answer Bran.
Wherever in the ranks the murmur ran
He'd find it—'You, there, whispering.
                    Up, you sneak,
Reactionary, eh? Come out and speak.'

33

"Then there'd be shrieks, a pistol shot, a cry,
And someone down. I was the third he caught.
The others pushed me out beneath his eye,
Saying, 'He's here; here, Captain.' Who'd
      have thought—
My old friends? But I know now. I've
      been taught. . . .
They cut away my two hands and my feet
And laughed and left me for the birds to eat.

34

"Oh, God's name! If I had my hands again
And Dymer here . . . it would not be my blood.
I am stronger now than he is, old with pain,
One grip would make him mine. But it's
      no good,
I'm dying fast. 'Look, Stranger,' where the wood
Grows lighter. It's the morning. Stranger dear,
Don't leave me. Talk a little while. Come near."

35

But Dymer, sitting hunched with knee
      to chin,
Close to the dying man, answered no word.
His face was stone. There was no meaning in
His wakeful eyes. Sometimes the other stirred
And fretted, near his death; and Dymer heard,
Yet sat like one that neither hears nor sees.
And the cold East whitened beyond the trees.

CANTO V

Dymer is wracked with guilt over the violence he caused and with grief over his lost love. He senses the beauty of nature all around him, but he wonders what it means, if anything. Wandering in the dark, he stumbles over a precipice and nearly falls to his death. Taking new strength from the glory of the natural world surrounding him, he resolves to push on.

CANTO V

1

THROUGH bearded cliffs a valley has
    driven thus deep
Its wedge into the mountain and no more.
The faint track of the farthest-wandering sheep
Ends here, and the grey hollows at their core
Of silence feel the dulled continuous roar
Of higher streams. At every step the skies
Grow less and in their place black ridges rise.

2

Hither, long after noon, with plodding tread
And eyes on earth, grown dogged,
    Dymer came,
Who all the long day in the woods had fled
From the horror of those lips that screamed
    his name
And cursed him. Busy wonder and
    keen shame
Were driving him, and little thoughts like bees
Followed and pricked him on and left no ease.

3

Now, when he looked and saw this emptiness
Seven times enfolded in the idle hills,
There came a chilly pause to his distress,
A cloud of the deep world-despair that fills
A man's heart like the incoming tide and kills
All pains except its own. In that broad sea
No hope, no change, and no regret can be.

4

He felt the eternal strength of the <u>silly</u> earth,
The unhastening circuit of the stars and sea,
The business of perpetual death and birth,
The meaningless precision. All must be
The same and still the same in each degree—
Who cared now? And he smiled and
        could forgive,
Believing that for sure he would not live.

Stanza 4

silly: in this context, solid

5

Then, where he saw a little water run
Beneath a bush, he slept. The chills of May
Came dropping and the stars peered one by one
Out of the deepening blue, while far away
The western brightness dulled to bars of grey.
Half-way to midnight, suddenly, from dreaming
He woke wide into present horror, screaming.

6

For he had dreamt of being in the arms
Of his beloved and in quiet places;
But all at once it filled with night alarms

And rapping guns: and men with
    splintered faces,
—No eyes, no nose, all red—were
    running races
With worms along the floor. And he ran out
To find the girl and shouted: and that shout

7

Had carried him into the waking world.
There stood the concave, vast, unfriendly night,
And over him the scroll of stars unfurled.
Then wailing like a child he rose upright,
Heart-sick with desolation. The new blight
Of loss had nipt him sore, and sad self-pity
Thinking of her—then thinking of the City.

8

For, in each moment's thought, the deeds
    of Bran,
The burning and the blood and his own shame,
Would tease him into madness till he ran
For refuge to the thought of her; whence came
Utter and endless loss—no, not a name,
Not a word, nothing left—himself alone
Crying amid that valley of old stone:

9

"How soon it all ran out! And I suppose
They, they up there, the old contriving powers,
They knew it all the time—for someone knows
And waits and watches till we pluck the flowers,
Then leaps. So soon—my store of happy hours

All gone before I knew. I have expended
My whole wealth in a day. It's finished, ended.

10

"And nothing left. Can it be possible
That <u>joy</u> flows through and, when the course
    is run,
It leaves no change, no mark on us to tell
Its passing? And as poor as we've begun
We end the richest day? What we have won,
Can it all die like this? . . . Joy flickers on
The razor-edge of the present and is gone.

Stanza 10

joy: Lewis often used the term *joy* in a specialized sense, connoting longing for the unattainable, an ache that was also an exquisite pleasure.

11

"What have I done to bear upon my name
The curse of Bran? I was not of his crew,
Nor any man's. And Dymer has the blame—
What have I done? Wronged whom?
    I never knew.
What's Bran to me? I had my deed to do
And ran out by myself, alone and free.
—Why should earth sing with joy and not for me?

12

"Ah, but the earth never did sing for joy. . . .
There is a glamour on the leaf and flower
And April comes and whistles to a boy
Over white fields: and, beauty has
    such power
Upon us, he believes her in that hour,
For who could not believe? Can it be false,
All that the blackbird says and the wind calls?

Stanza 13

eyebright: wild herb with flowers on long stalks

13

"What have I done? No living thing I made
Nor wished to suffer harm. I sought my good
Because the spring was gloriously arrayed
And the blue <u>eyebright</u> misted all the wood.
Yet to obey that springtime and my blood,
This was to be unarmed and off my guard
And gave God time to hit once and hit hard.

14

"The men built right who made that City of ours,
They knew their world. A man must crouch
    to face
Infinite malice, watching at all hours,
Shut Nature out—give her no moment's space
For entry. The first needs of all our race
Are walls, a den, a cover. Traitor I
Who first ran out beneath the open sky.

15

"Our fortress and fenced place I made to fall,
I slipt the sentries and let in the foe.
I have lost my brothers and my love and all.
Nothing is left but me. Now let me go.
I have seen the world stripped naked and I know.
Great God, take back your world. I will have none
Of all your glittering gauds but death alone."

16

Meanwhile the earth swung round in
    hollow night.
Souls without number in all nations slept

Snug on her back, safe speeding towards
    the light;
Hours tolled, and in damp woods the night
    beast crept,
And over the long seas the watch was kept
In black ships, twinkling onward, green
    and red:
Always the ordered stars moved overhead.

17

And no one knew that <u>Dymer in his scales</u>
Had weighed all these and found them
    nothing worth.
Indifferently the dawn that never fails
Troubled the east of night with gradual birth,
Whispering a change of colours on
    cold earth,
And a bird woke, then two. The sunlight ran
Along the hills and yellow day began.

Stanza 17

Dymer in his scales: Daniel
5:27: "You have been weighed
on the scales and found
wanting." (NIV)

18

But stagnant gloom clung in the valley yet;
Hills crowded out a third part of the sky,
Black-looking, and the boulders dripped
    with wet:
No bird sang. Dymer, shivering, heaved
    a sigh
And yawned and said: "It's cruel work to die
Of hunger"; and again, with cloudy breath
Blown between chattering teeth, "It's a
    bad death."

Stanza 19

NB: "Gulley's" was changed to "gully's" in *Narrative Poems* (1972).

19

He crouched and clasped his hands about
    his knees
And hugged his own limbs for the pitiful sense
Of homeliness they had—familiars these,
This body, at least, his own, his last defence.
But soon his morning misery drove him thence,
Eating his heart, to wander as chance led
On, upward, to the narrowing gulley's head.

20

The cloud lay on the nearest mountain-top
As from a giant's chimney smoking there,
But Dymer took no heed. Sometimes he'd stop,
Sometimes he hurried faster, as despair
Pricked deeper, and cried out: "Even now,
    somewhere,
Bran with his crew's at work. They rack,
    they burn,
And there's no help in me. I've served their turn."

21

Stanza 21

vanguard: the leading units in an advancing army

combes: steep valleys

Meanwhile the furrowed fog rolled
    down ahead,
Long tatters of its vanguard smearing round
The bases of the crags. Like cobweb shed
Down the deep combes it dulled the
    tinkling sound
Of water on the hills. The spongy ground
Faded three yards ahead: then nearer yet
Fell the cold wreaths, the white depth
    gleaming wet.

22

Then after a long time the path he trod
Led downward. Then all suddenly it dipped
Far steeper, and yet steeper, with smooth sod.
He was half running now. A stone that slipped
Beneath him, rattled headlong down:
      he tripped,
Stumbled and clutched—then panic,
      and no hope
To stop himself, once lost upon that slope.

23

And faster, ever faster, and his eye
Caught tree-tops far below. The
      nightmare feeling
Had gripped him. He was screaming: and
      the sky
Seemed hanging upside down. Then
      struggling, reeling,
With effort beyond thought he hung
      half kneeling,
Halted one saving moment. With wild will
He clawed into the hillside and lay still,

24

Half hanging on both arms. His idle feet
Dangled and found no hold. The moor lay wet
Against him and he sweated with the heat
Of terror, all alive. His teeth were set.
"By God, I will not die," said he; "not yet."
Then slowly, slowly, with enormous strain,
He heaved himself an inch: then heaved again,

25

Till saved and spent he lay. He felt indeed
It was the big, round world beneath his breast,
The mother planet proven at his need.
The shame of glad surrender stood confessed,
He cared not for his boasts. This, this was best,
This giving up of all. He need not strive;
He panted, he lay still, he was alive.

26

And now his eyes were closed. Perhaps he slept,
Lapt in unearthly quiet—never knew
How bit by bit the fog's white rearguard crept
Over the crest and faded, and the blue
First brightening at the zenith trembled through,
And deepening shadows took a sharper form
Each moment, and the sandy earth grew warm.

27

Yet, dreaming of blue skies, in dream he heard
The pure voice of a lark that seemed to send
Its song from heights beyond all height.
That bird
Sang out of heaven, "The world will never end,"
Sang from the gates of heaven, "Will never end,"
Sang till it seemed there was no other thing
But bright space and one voice set there to sing.

28

It seemed to be the murmur and the voice
Of beings beyond number, each and all
Singing I AM. Each of itself made choice

And was: whence flows the justice that men call
Divine. She keeps the great worlds lest they fall
From hour to hour, and makes the hills renew
Their ancient youth and sweetens all
      things through.

29

It seemed to be the low voice of the world
Brooding alone beneath the strength of things,
Murmuring of days and nights and
      years unfurled
Forever, and the unwearied joy that brings
Out of old fields the flowers of unborn springs,
Out of old wars and cities burned with wrong,
A splendour in the dark, a tale, a song.

30

The dream ran thin towards waking, and
      he knew
It was but a bird's piping with no sense.
He rolled round on his back. The sudden blue,
Quivering with light, hard, cloudless
      and intense,
Shone over him. The lark still sounded thence
And stirred him at the heart. Some
      spacious thought
Was passing by too gently to be caught.

31

With that he thrust the damp hair from his face
And sat upright. The perilous cliff
      dropped sheer

Before him, close at hand, and from his place
Listening in mountain silence he could hear
Birds crying far below. It was not fear
That took him, but strange glory, when his eye
Looked past the edge into surrounding sky.

32
He rose and stood. Then lo! the world beneath
—Wide pools that in the sun-splashed
      foothills lay,
Sheep-dotted downs, soft-piled, and
      rolling heath,
River and shining weir and steeples grey
And the green waves of forest. Far away
Distance rose heaped on distance: nearer hand,
The white roads leading down to a new land.

CANTO VI

*Dymer finds his way down into a green valley and
hears a lark singing, but then the crack of a rifle. He
meets an old man dressed like a wizard, whose house
is surrounded by thick hedges, as if he is trying to keep
nature out. The old man explains that he killed the
lark because he considered its singing a distraction.
Dymer eats, sleeps deeply, and then tells the magician
his story—the revolution he caused and the mysterious lover he lost. The magician speculates that the
woman was a spirit, and that the palace itself may
have been an illusion. He tells Dymer that the best
cure for broken dreams is to dream even more deeply.*

*Dymer is wary of the old man's fascination with all
things occult, and he still doesn't understand why he
would kill an innocent songbird.*

CANTO VI

1

THE sun was high in heaven and Dymer stood
   A bright speck on the endless mountain-side,
Till, blossom after blossom, that rich mood
Faded and truth rolled homeward, like a tide
Before whose edge the weak soul fled to hide
In vain, with ostrich head, through
          many a shape
Of coward fancy, whimpering for escape.

2

But only for a moment; then his soul
Took the full swell and heaved a dripping prow
Clear of the shattering wave-crest. He was whole.
No veils should hide the truth, no truth
          should cow
The dear self-pitying heart. "I'll babble now
No longer," Dymer said. "I'm broken in.
Pack up the dreams and let the life begin."

3

With this he turned. "I must have food to-day,"
He muttered. Then among the cloudless hills
By winding tracks he sought the downward way
And followed the steep course of tumbling rills
—Came to the glens the wakening
          mountain fills

In springtime with the echoing splash and shock
Of waters leaping cold from rock to rock.

4

And still, it seemed, that lark with its refrain
Sang in the sky, and wind was in his hair
And hope at heart. Then once, and once again,
He heard a gun fired off. It broke the air
As a stone breaks a pond, and everywhere
The dry crags echoed clear: and at the sound
Once a big bird rose whirring from the ground.

5

In half an hour he reached the level land
And followed the field-paths and crossed
      the stiles,
Then looked and saw, near by, on his left hand
An old house, folded round with billowy piles
Of dark yew hedge. The moss was on the tiles,
The pigeons in the yard, and in the tower
A clock that had no hands and told no hour.

6

He hastened. In warm waves the garden scent
Came stronger at each stride. The mountain
      breeze
Was gone. He reached the gates; then in he went
And seemed to lose the sky—such weight
      of trees
Hung overhead. He heard the noise of bees
And saw, far off, in the blue shade between
The windless elms, one walking on the green.

7

It was a mighty man whose beardless face
Beneath grey hair shone out so large and mild
It made a sort of moonlight in the place.
A dreamy desperation, wistful-wild,
Showed in his glance and gait: yet like a child,
An Asian emperor's only child, was he
With his grave looks and bright solemnity.

8

And over him there hung the witching air,
The wilful courtesy, of the days of old,
The graces wherein idleness grows fair;
And somewhat in his sauntering walk he rolled
And toyed about his waist with seals of gold,
Or stood to ponder often in mid-stride,
Tilting his heavy head upon one side.

9

When Dymer had called twice, he turned his eye:
Then, coming out of silence (as a star
All in one moment slips into the sky
Of evening, yet we feel it comes from far),
He said, "Sir, you are welcome. Few there are
That come my way": and in huge hands
        he pressed
Dymer's cold hand and bade him in to rest.

10

"How did you find this place out? Have
        you heard
My gun? It was but now I killed a lark."

Stanza 7

It was a mighty man: In his 1950 preface, Lewis says that the magician's physical appearance resembles that of the Irish poet W. B. Yeats (1865–1939). Actually, the resemblance goes deeper than that. Lewis met Yeats in Oxford in March 1921 and thought that Yeats was becoming more magician than poet, given all his talk of spiritualism, the Kabbalah, and other occult topics.

Stanza 10

I killed a lark: Killing a harmless songbird is, of course, an act of gratuitous violence. In Lewis's books, people who shoot guns are morally obtuse characters. For example, in *Out of the Silent Planet*, Weston needlessly kills an innocent Malacandran creature. In *The Magician's Nephew*, Uncle Andrew wishes he had a gun so he could shoot at Aslan himself. Lewis's villains do not see any sanctity in life, either animal or human. In *The Abolition of Man* (1943) Lewis argued that magic and applied science are twins, both attempts to subdue reality to the wishes of men. The Magician tries to use *both* schemes of mastery: technology (the gun) and magic (the potions) to impose his will on others.

"What, Sir!" said Dymer; "shoot the
    singing bird?"
"Sir," said the man, "they sing from dawn
    till dark,
And interrupt my dreams too long. But hark . . .
Another? Did you hear no singing? No?
It was my fancy, then . . . pray, let it go.

11

"From here you see my garden's only flaw.
Stand here, Sir, at the dial." Dymer stood.
The Master pointed; then he looked and saw
How hedges and the funeral quietude
Of black trees fringed the garden like a wood,
And only, in one place, one gap that showed
The blue side of the hills, the white hill-road.

12

"I have planted fir and larch to fill the gap,"
He said, "because this too makes war upon
The art of dream. But by some great mishap
Nothing I plant will grow there. We pass on. . . .
The sunshine of the afternoon is gone.
Let us go in. It draws near time to sup
—I hate the garden till the moon is up."

13

They passed from the hot lawn into the gloom
And coolness of the porch: then, past a door
That opened with no noise, into a room
Where green leaves choked the window and
    the floor

Sank lower than the ground. A tattered store
Of brown books met the eye: a crystal ball:
And masks with empty eyes along the wall.

14

Then Dymer sat, but knew not how nor where,
And supper was set out before these two,
—He saw not how—with silver old and rare
But tarnished. And he ate and never knew
What meats they were. At every bite he grew
More drowsy and let slide his crumbling will.
The Master at his side was talking still.

15

And all his talk was tales of magic words
And of the nations in the clouds above,
<u>Astral and aerish</u> tribes who fish for birds
With angles. And by history he could prove
How chosen spirits from earth had won
    their love,
As Arthur, or <u>Usheen</u>: and to their isle
Went Helen for the sake of a Greek smile.

16

And ever in his talk he mustered well
His texts and strewed old authors round the way,
"Thus <u>Wierus</u> writes," and "Thus the
    <u>Hermetics</u> tell,"
"This was <u>Agrippa's</u> view," and "Others say
With <u>Cardan</u>," till he had stolen quite away
Dymer's dull wits and softly drawn apart
The ivory gates of hope that change the heart.

Stanza 15

Astral and aerish tribes: In occult studies, spirit-bodies may travel to planes of being beyond the physical world.

Usheen: Ossian, legendary poet of Ireland who wrote about visiting Tir na nÓg ("the land of the young")

Stanza 16

Wierus: Johann Weyer, Dutch occultist

Hermetics: Esoteric philosophy seeking hidden truth behind all religions.

Agrippa: Cornelius Agrippa (1486–1535), German theologian and occultist. The magician and tutor Doctor Cornelius in *Prince Caspian* is probably named after him.

Cardan: Girolamo Cardan (1501–1576), Italian mathematician who wrote an influential book on algebra.

17

Dymer was talking now. Now Dymer told
Of his own love and losing, drowsily.
The Master leaned towards him, "Was it cold,
This spirit, to the touch?"—"No, Sir, not she,"
Said Dymer. And his host: "Why this must be
Aethereal, not aerial! O my soul,
Be still . . . but wait. Tell on, Sir, tell the whole."

18

Then Dymer told him of the beldam too,
The old, old, matriarchal dreadfulness.
Over the Master's face a shadow drew,
He shifted in his chair and "Yes" and "Yes,"
He murmured twice. "I never looked for less!
Always the same . . . that frightful woman shape
Besets the dream-way and the soul's escape."

19

But now when Dymer made to talk of Bran,
A huge indifference fell upon his host,
Patient and wandering-eyed. Then he began,
"Forgive me. You are young. What helps us most
Is to find out again that heavenly ghost
Who loves you. For she was a ghost, and you
In that place where you met were ghostly too.

20

"Listen! for I can launch you on the stream
Will roll you to the shores of her own land. . . .
I could be sworn you never learned to dream,
But every night you take with careless hand

What chance may bring? I'll teach you
    to command
The comings and the goings of your spirit
Through all that borderland which
    dreams inherit.

21

"You shall have hauntings suddenly. And often,
When you forget, when least you think of her
(For so you shall forget), a light will soften
Over the evening woods. And in the stir
Of morning dreams (oh, I will teach you, Sir)
There'll come a sound of wings. Or you shall be
Waked in the midnight murmuring, 'It was she.'"

22

"No, no," said Dymer, "not that way. I seem
To have slept for twenty years. Now—while
    I shake
Out of my eyes that dust of burdening dream,
Now when the long clouds tremble ripe to break
And the far hills appear, when first I wake,
Still blinking, struggling towards the world
    of men,
And longing—would you turn me back again?

23

"Dreams? I have had my dream too long.
    I thought
The sun rose for my sake. I ran down blind
And dancing to the abyss. Oh, Sir, I brought
Boy-laughter for a gift to gods who find

The martyr's soul too soft. But that's behind.
I'm waking now. They broke me. All ends thus
Always—and we're for them, not they for us.

24

"And she—she was no dream. It would be waste
To seek her there, the living in that den
Of lies." The Master smiled. "You are in haste!
For broken dreams the cure is, Dream again
And deeper. If the waking world, and men,
And nature marred your dream—so much
          the worse
For a crude world beneath its <u>primal curse</u>."

25

—"Ah, but you do not know! Can dreams
          do this,
Pluck out blood-guiltiness upon the shore
Of memory—and undo what's done amiss,
And bid the thing that has been be no more?"
—"Sir, it is only dreams unlock that door,"
He answered with a shrug. "What would
          you have?
In dreams the thrice-proved coward can
          feel brave.

26

"In dreams the fool is free from scorning voices.
Grey-headed whores are virgin there again.
Out of the past dream brings long-buried
          choices,
All in a moment snaps the tenfold chain

That life took years in forging. There the stain
Of oldest sins—how do the good words go?—
Though they were scarlet, shall be <u>white as snow</u>."

Stanza 26

white as snow: Isaiah 1:18,
"Though your sins be as scarlet,
they shall be as white as snow."

27

Then, drawing near, when Dymer did not speak,
"My little son," said he, "your wrong and right
Are also dreams: fetters to bind the weak
Faster to phantom earth and blear the sight.
Wake into dreams, into the larger light
That quenches these frail stars. They will
        not know
Earth's bye-laws in the land to which you go."

28

—"I must undo my sins."—"An earthly law,
And, even in earth, the child of yesterday.
Throw down your human pity; cast your awe
Behind you; put repentance all away.
Home to the elder depths! for never they
Supped with the stars who dared not
        <u>slough behind</u>
The last shred of earth's holies from their mind."

Stanza 28

slough behind: cast off

29

"Sir," answered Dymer, "I would be content
To drudge in earth, easing my
        heart's disgrace,
Counting a year's long service lightly spent
If once at the year's end I saw her face
Somewhere, being then most weary, in
        some place

I looked not for that joy—or heard her near
Whispering, 'Yet courage, friend,' for one
    more year."

30

"Pish," said the Master. "Will you have the truth?
You think that virtue saves? Her people care
For the high heart and idle hours of youth;
For these they will descend our lower air,
Not virtue. You would nerve your arm and bear
Your burden among men? Look to it, child:
By virtue's self vision can be defiled.

31

"You will grow full of pity and the love of men,
And toil until the morning moisture dries
Out of your heart. Then once, or once again,
It may be you will find her: but your eyes
Soon will be grown too dim. The task that lies
Next to your hand will hide her. You shall be
The child of earth and gods you shall not see."

32

Here suddenly he ceased. Tip-toes he went.
A bolt clicked—then the window
    creaked ajar,
And out of the wet world the hedgerow scent
Came floating; and the dark without one star
Nor shape of trees nor sense of near and far,
The undimensioned night and formless skies
Were there, and were the Master's great allies.

33

"I am very old," he said. "But if the time
We suffered in our dreams were counted age,
I have outlived the ocean and my prime
Is with me to this day. Years cannot gauge
The dream-life. In the turning of a page,
Dozing above my book, I have lived through
More ages than the lost <u>Lemuria</u> knew.

Stanza 33

Lemuria: legendary lost
continent in the Indian or
Pacific Ocean

34

"I am not mortal. Were I doomed to die
This hour, in this half-hour I interpose
A thousand years of dream: and, those gone by,
As many more, and in the last of those,
Ten thousand—ever journeying towards
        a close
That I shall never reach: for time shall flow,
Wheel within wheel, interminably slow.

35

"And you will drink my cup and go your way
Into the valley of dreams. You have heard
        the call.
Come hither and escape. Why should you stay?
Earth is a sinking ship, a house whose wall
Is tottering while you sweep; the roof will fall
Before the work is done. You cannot mend it.
Patch as you will, at last the rot must end it."

Stanza 36

Atlas: In Greek mythology, the
titan condemned to hold up
the heavens on his shoulders.
Lewis follows the common
idea that Atlas held up the
world, but the ancients
specified it was the heavens
that he shouldered for eternity.

36

Then Dymer lifted up his heavy head
Like <u>Atlas</u> on broad shoulders bearing up

The insufferable globe. "I had not said,"
He mumbled, "never said I'd taste the cup.
What, is it this you give me? Must I sup?
Oh, lies, all lies. . . . Why did you kill the lark?
Guide me the cup to lip . . . it is so dark."

CANTO VII

*As Dymer sleeps and dreams, the magician is alone
with his thoughts. He knows that his promises of en-
chanted dreams are lies, and that he himself has
become ensnared in his own esoteric practices. He
sleeps little now and dreads the spirits that possess
him almost like demons. Dymer awakens and recounts his dream. He dreamed he saw a great bear,
emerald birds, and finally his lover. She tries to seduce
him, but Dymer realizes that all this is dream and
illusion, an expression of his own desires, fears, and
lusts. He takes a drink of water to clear his head, then
jumps out the window to escape the magician. The
latter shoots at Dymer as he is fleeing, wounding him.*

CANTO VII

1

THE host had trimmed his lamp. The
        downy moth
Came from the garden. Where the
        lamplight shed
Its circle of smooth white upon the cloth,
Down mid the rinds of fruit and broken bread,

Upon his sprawling arms lay Dymer's head;
And often, as he dreamed, he shifted place,
Muttering and showing half his drunken face.

2

The beating stillness of the dead of night
Flooded the room. The dark and sleepy powers
Settled upon the house and filled it quite;
Far from the roads it lay, from belfry towers
And hen-roosts, in a world of folded flowers,
Buried in loneliest fields where beasts that love
The silence through the unrustled
  hedgerows move.

3

Now from the Master's lips there breathed a sigh
As of a man released from some control
That wronged him. Without aim his
  wandering eye,
Unsteadied and unfixed, began to roll.
His lower lip dropped loose. The informing soul
Seemed fading from his face. He laughed
  out loud
Once only: then looked round him, hushed
  and cowed.

4

Then, summoning all himself, with
  tightened lip,
With desperate coolness and attentive air,
He touched between his thumb and
  finger-tip,

Each in its turn, the four legs of his chair,
Then back again in haste—there!—that one there
Had been forgotten . . . once more! . . .
        safer now;
That's better! and he smiled and cleared his brow.

5

Yet this was but a moment's ease. Once more
He glanced about him like a startled hare,
His big eyes bulged with horror. As before,
Quick!—to the touch that saves him. But despair
Is nearer by one step; and in his chair
Huddling he waits. He knows that they'll
        come strong
Again and yet again and all night long;

6

And after this night comes another night
—Night after night until the worst of all.
And now too even the noonday and the light
Let through the horrors. Oh, could he recall
The deep sleep and the dreams that used to fall
Around him for the asking! But, somehow,
Something's amiss . . . sleep comes so
        rarely now.

7

Stanza 7

dog returning to its vomit:
Proverbs 26:11, "As a dog
returneth to his vomit, so a fool
returneth to his folly."

Then, like the dog returning to its vomit,
He staggered to the bookcase to renew
Yet once again the taint he had taken from it,
And shuddered as he went. But horror drew
His feet, as joy draws others. There in view

Was his strange heaven and his far
    stranger hell,
His secret lust, his soul's dark citadel:—

8

Old <u>Theomagia</u>, Demonology,
<u>Cabbala</u>, Chemic Magic, <u>Book of the Dead</u>,
Damning <u>Hermetic rolls</u> that none may see
Save the already damned—such grubs are bred
From minds that lose the Spirit and seek instead
For spirits in the dust of dead men's error,
Buying the joys of dream with dreamland terror.

9

This lost soul looked them over one and all,
Now sickening at the heart's root; for he knew
This night was one of those when he would fall
And scream alone (such things they made
    him do)
And roll upon the floor. The madness grew
Wild at his breast, but still his brain was clear
That he could watch the moment coming near.

10

But, ere it came, he heard a sound, half groan,
Half muttering, from the table. Like a child
Caught unawares that thought it was alone,
He started as in guilt. His gaze was wild,
Yet pitiably with all his will he smiled,
—So strong is shame, even then.
    And Dymer stirred,
Now waking, and looked up and spoke one word:

Stanza 8

Theomagia: A three-volume book of nearly a thousand pages written by John Heydon (1629–1667), an English Rosicrucian, astrologer, and occult philosopher.

Cabbala: A medieval book of Jewish mystical teachings and esoteric rabbinic doctrines. There are numerous variant spellings of Kabbalah. Lewis used one of these, Cabbala, in this poem. However, the most accepted current usage is spelled Kabbalah.

Book of the Dead: Ancient Egyptian book of spells used to guide the recently deceased in the afterlife.

Hermetic rolls: Esoteric scrolls of magic and astrology.

11

"Water!" he said. He was too dazed to see
What hell-wrung face looked down, what
    shaking hand
Poured out the draught. He drank it thirstily
And held the glass for more. "Your land . . .
    your land
Of dreams," he said. "All lies! . . .
    I understand
More than I did. Yes, water. I've the thirst
Of hell itself. Your magic's all accursed."

12

When he had drunk again he rose and stood,
Pallid and cold with sleep. "By God," he said,
"You did me wrong to send me to that wood.
I sought a living spirit and found instead
Bogies and wraiths." The Master raised his head,
Calm as a sage, and answered, "Are you mad?
Come, sit you down. Tell me what dream
    you had."

13

—"I dreamed about a wood . . . an autumn red
Of beech-trees big as mountains.
    Down between—
The first thing that I saw—a clearing spread,
Deep down, oh, very deep. Like some ravine
Or like a well it sank, that forest green
Under its weight of forest—more remote
Than one ship in a landlocked sea afloat.

14

"Then through the narrowed sky some
     heavy bird
Would flap its way, a stillness more profound
Following its languid wings. Sometimes
     I heard
Far off in the long woods with quiet sound
The sudden chestnut thumping to the ground,
Or the dry leaf that drifted past upon
Its endless loiter earthward and was gone.

15

"Then next . . . I heard twigs splintering on
     my right
And rustling in the thickets. Turning there
I watched. Out of the foliage came in sight
The head and blundering shoulders of a bear,
Glistening in sable black, with beady stare
Of eyes towards me, and no room to fly
—But padding soft and slow the beast came by.

16

"And—mark their flattery—stood and rubbed
     his flank
Against me. On my shaken legs I felt
His heart beat. And my hand that stroked
     him sank
Wrist-deep upon his shoulder in soft pelt.
Yes . . . and across my spirit as I smelt
The wild thing's scent, a new, sweet wildness ran
Whispering of Eden-fields long lost by man.

17

"So far was well. But then came emerald birds
Singing about my head. I took my way
Sauntering the cloistered woods. Then came
    the herds,
The roebuck and the fallow deer at play,
Trooping to nose my hand. All this, you say,
Was sweet? Oh, sweet! . . . do you think I
    could not see
That beasts and wood were nothing else but me?

18

Stanza 18

brake: thicket

" . . . That I was making everything I saw,
Too sweet, far too well fitted to desire
To be a living thing? Those forests draw
No sap from the kind earth: the solar fire
And soft rain feed them not: that fairy brier
Pricks not: the birds sing sweetly in that <u>brake</u>
Not for their own delight but for my sake!

19

"It is a world of sad, cold, heartless stuff,
Like a bought smile, no joy in it."—"But stay;
Did you not find your lady?"—"Sure enough!
I still had hopes till then. The autumn day
Was westering, the long shadows crossed my way,
When over daisies folded for the night
Beneath rook-gathering elms she came in sight."

20

—"Was she not fair?"—"So beautiful, she seemed
Almost a living soul. But every part

Was what I made it—all that I had dreamed—
No more, no less: the mirror of my heart,
Such things as boyhood feigns beneath
    the smart
Of solitude and spring. I was deceived
Almost. In that first moment I believed.

21

"For a big, brooding rapture, tense as fire
And calm as a first sleep, had soaked me through
Without thought, without word,
    without desire. . . .
Meanwhile above our heads the deepening blue
Burnished the gathering stars. Her
    sweetness drew
A veil before my eyes. The minutes passed
Heavy like loaded vines. She spoke at last.

22

"She said, for this land only did men love
The shadow-lands of earth. All our disease
Of longing, all the hopes we fabled of,
Fortunate islands or <u>Hesperian seas</u>
Or woods beyond the West, were but the breeze
That blew from off those shores: one far,
    spent breath
That reached even to the world of change
    and death.

Stanza 22

Hesperian seas: In the west, in Greek mythology, Hesperides was a western garden of trees with golden apples, guarded by a dragon. Lewis developed this imagery much more fully in *Perelandra*.

23

"She told me I had journeyed home at last
Into the golden age and the good countrie

That had been always there. She bade me cast
My cares behind forever:—on her knee
Worshipped me, lord and love—oh, I can see
Her red lips even now! Is it not wrong
That men's delusions should be made so strong?

24

"For listen, I was so <u>besotted</u> now
  She made me think that I was somehow seeing
The very core of truth . . . I felt somehow,
  Beyond all veils, the inward pulse of being.
Thought was enslaved, but oh, it felt
        like freeing
And draughts of larger air. It is too much!
Who can come through untainted from
        that touch?

25

"There I was nearly wrecked. But mark the rest:
  She went too fast. Soft to my arms she came.
The robe slipped from her shoulder. The
        smooth breast
Was bare against my own. She shone like flame
Before me in the dusk, all love, all shame—
Faugh!—and it was myself. But all was well,
For, at the least, that moment snapped the spell.

26

"As when you light a candle, the great gloom
Which was the unbounded night, sinks down,
        compressed
To four white walls in one familiar room,

So the vague joy shrank wilted in my breast
And narrowed to one point, unmasked,
    confessed;
Fool's paradise was gone: instead was there
King Lust with his black, sudden, serious stare.

27

"That moment in a cloud among the trees
Wild music and the glare of torches came.
On sweated faces, on the prancing knees
Of shaggy <u>satyrs</u> fell the smoky flame,
On ape and goat and crawlers without name,
On rolling breast, black eyes and tossing hair,
On old bald-headed witches, lean and bare.

Stanza 27

satyrs: In Greek mythology, a woodland creature with the pointed ears, shaggy legs, and the short horns of a goat, associated with lechery and revelry.

28

"They beat the devilish tom-tom rub-a-dub;
Lunging, leaping, in unwieldy romp,
Singing <u>Cotytto</u> and <u>Beelzebub</u>,
With devil-dancers' mask and phallic pomp,
Torn raw with briers and caked from
    many a swamp,
They came, among the wild flowers
    dripping blood
And churning the green mosses into mud.

Stanza 28

Cotytto: Orgiastic ritual associated with Kotys, the goddess of sexuality

Beelzebub: Philistine god whom Christians came to consider the name of a demon, "Lord of the Flies"

29

"They sang, 'Return! Return! We are the lust
That was before the world and still shall be
When your last law is trampled into dust,
We are the mother swamp, the primal sea
Whence the dry land appeared. Old, old are we.

It is but a return . . . it's nothing new,
Easy as slipping on a well-worn shoe.'

30

"And then there came warm mouths
and finger-tips
Preying upon me, whence I could not see,
Then . . . a huge face, low browed,
with swollen lips
Crooning, 'I am not beautiful as she,
But I'm the older love; you shall love me
Far more than Beauty's self. You have been ours
Always. We are the world's most ancient powers.'

31

"First flatterer and then bogy—like a dream!
Sir, are you listening? Do you also know
How close to the soft laughter comes the scream
Down yonder?" But his host cried sharply, "No.
Leave me alone. Why will you plague me? Go!
Out of my house! Begone!"—"With all
my heart,"
Said Dymer. "But one word before we part."

32

He paused, and in his cheek the
anger burned:
Then turning to the table, he poured out
More water. But before he drank he turned—
Then leaped back to the window with a shout
For there—it was no dream—beyond
all doubt

He saw the Master crouch with levelled gun,
Cackling in maniac voice, "Run, Dymer, run!"

33
He ducked and sprang far out.
    The starless night
On the wet lawn closed round him every way.
Then came the gun-crack and the splash of light
Vanished as soon as seen. Cool garden clay
Slid from his feet. He had fallen and he lay
Face downward among leaves—then up and on
Through branch and leaf till sense and breath
      were gone.

CANTO VIII

*Dymer lies in a country lane, struggling with the pain
from his bullet wound. His lover appears yet again, ex-
plaining that she is a spirit, a kind of wish-fulfillment
dream. Dymer asks her, "Has heaven no voice to help?
Must things of dust guess their own way in the dark?"
She answers simply, "They must." After she is gone,
Dymer makes his way to a belfried tower, opening a
wooden gate and finding himself in a cemetery.*

CANTO VIII

1
W HEN next he found himself no house
    was there,
No garden and great trees. Beside a lane

In grass he lay. Now first he was aware
That, all one side, his body glowed with pain:
And the next moment and the next again
Was neither less nor more. Without a pause
It clung like a great beast with fastened claws;

2

Stanza 2

ogre: legendary monster, often
said to eat humans

That for a time he could not frame a thought
Nor know himself for self, nor pain for pain,
Till moment added on to moment taught
The new, strange art of living on that plane,
Taught how the grappled soul must still remain,
Still choose and think and understand beneath
The very grinding of the ogre's teeth.

3

He heard the wind along the hedges sweep,
The quarter striking from a neighbouring tower.
About him was the weight of the world's sleep;
Within, the thundering pain. That quiet hour
Heeded it not. It throbbed, it raged with power
Fit to convulse the heavens: and at his side
The soft peace drenched the meadows far
                    and wide.

4

The air was cold, the earth was cold with dew,
The hedge behind him dark as ink. But now
The clouds broke and a paler heaven
                    showed through
Spacious with sudden stars, breathing somehow
The sense of change to slumbering lands. A cow

Coughed in the fields behind. The
    puddles showed
Like pools of sky amid the darker road.

5

And he could see his own limbs faintly white
And the blood black upon them. Then by chance
He turned . . . and it was strange: there at
    his right
He saw a woman standing, and her glance
Met his: and at the meeting his deep trance
Changed not, and while he looked the
    knowledge grew
She was not of the old life but the new.

6

"Who is it?" he said. "The loved one,
    the long lost."
He stared upon her. "Truly?"—"Truly indeed."
—"Oh, lady, you come late. I am tempest-tossed,
Broken and wrecked. I am dying. Look, I bleed.
Why have you left me thus and given no heed
To all my prayers?—left me to be the game
Of all deceits?"—"You should have asked
    my name."

7

—"What are you, then?" But to his sudden cry
She did not answer. When he had
    thought awhile
He said: "How can I tell it is no lie?
It may be one more phantom to beguile

The brain-sick dreamer with its harlot smile."
"I have not smiled," she said. The
        neighbouring bell
Tolled out another quarter. Silence fell.

8

And after a long pause he spoke again:
"Leave me," he said. "Why do you watch with me?
You do not love me. Human tears and pain
And hoping for the things that cannot be,
And blundering in the night where none
        can see,
And courage with cold back against the wall,
You do not understand."—"I know them all.

9

"The gods themselves know pain, the
        eternal forms.
In realms beyond the reach of cloud, and skies
Nearest the ends of air, where come no storms
Nor sound of earth, I have looked into
        their eyes
Peaceful and filled with pain beyond surmise,
Filled with an ancient woe man cannot reach
One moment though in fire; yet calm
        their speech."

10

"Then these," said Dymer, "were the world
        I wooed . . .
These were the holiness of flowers and grass
And desolate dews . . . these, the eternal mood

Blowing the eternal theme through men
    that pass.
I called myself their lover—I that was
Less fit for that long service than the least
Dull, workday drudge of men or faithful beast.

11

"Why do they lure to them such spirits as mine,
The weak, the passionate, and the fool of dreams?
When better men go safe and never pine
With whisperings at the heart, soul-sickening
    gleams
Of infinite desire, and joy that seems
The promise of full power? For it was they,
The gods themselves, that led me on this way.

12

"Give me the truth! I ask not now for pity.
When gods call, can the following them be sin?
Was it false light that lured me from the City?
Where was the path—without it or within?
Must it be one blind throw to lose or win?
Has heaven no voice to help? Must things
    of dust
Guess their own way in the dark?" She said,
    "They must."

13

Another silence: then he cried in wrath,
"You came in human shape, in sweet disguise
Wooing me, lurking for me in my path,
Hid your eternal cold with woman's eyes,

Snared me with shows of love—and all was lies."
She answered, "For our kind must come to all
If bidden, but in the shape for which they call."

14

"What!" answered Dymer. "Do you change
    and sway
To serve us, as the obedient planets spin
About the sun? Are you but potter's clay
For us to mould—unholy to our sin
And holy to the holiness within?"
She said, "Waves fall on many an unclean shore,
Yet the salt seas are holy as before.

15

"Our nature is no purer for the saint
That worships, nor from him that uses ill
Our beauty can we suffer any taint.
As from the first we were, so are we still:
With incorruptibles the mortal will
Corrupts itself, and clouded eyes will make
Darkness within from beams they cannot take."

16

"Well . . . it is well," said Dymer. "If I have used
The embreathing spirit amiss . . . what would
    have been
The strength of all my days I have refused
And plucked the stalk, too hasty, in the green,
Trusted the good for best, and having seen
Half-beauty, or beauty's fringe, the lowest stair,
The common incantation, worshipped there."

17

But presently he cried in his great pain,
"If I had loved a beast it would repay,
But I have loved the Spirit and loved in vain.
Now let me die . . . ah, but before the way
Is ended quite, in the last hour of day,
Is there no word of comfort, no one kiss
Of human love? Does it all end in this?"

18

She answered, "Never ask of life and death.
Uttering these names you dream of wormy clay
Or of surviving ghosts. This withering breath
Of words is the beginning of decay
In truth, when truth grows cold and pines away
Among the ancestral images. Your eyes
First see her dead: and more, the more she dies.

19

"You are still dreaming, dreams you shall forget
When you have cast your fetters, far from here.
Go forth; the journey is not ended yet.
You have seen Dymer dead and on the bier
More often than you dream and dropped no tear,
You have slain him every hour. Think not at all
Of death lest into death by thought you fall."

20

He turned to question her, then looked again,
And lo! the shape was gone. The darkness lay
Heavy as yet and a cold, shifting rain
Fell with the breeze that springs before the day.

It was an hour death loves. Across the way
The clock struck once again. He saw near by
The black shape of the tower against the sky.

21

Meanwhile above the torture and the riot
Of leaping pulse and nerve that shot with pain,
Somewhere aloof and poised in spectral quiet
His soul was thinking on. The dizzied brain
Scarce seemed her organ: link by link the chain
That bound him to the flesh was loosening fast
And the new life breathed in unmoved and vast.

22

"It was like this," he thought—"like this,
    or worse,
For him that I found bleeding in the wood . . .
Blessings upon him . . . there I learned the curse
That rests on Dymer's name, and truth
    was good.
He has forgotten now the fire and blood,
He has forgotten that there was a man
Called Dymer. He knows not himself nor Bran.

23

"How long have I been moved at heart in vain
About this Dymer, thinking this was I . . .
Why did I follow close his joy and pain
More than another man's? For he will die,
The little cloud will vanish and the sky
Reign as before. The stars remain and earth
And Man, as in the years before my birth.

24

"There was a Dymer once who worked
    and played
About the City; I sloughed him off and ran.
There was a Dymer in the forest glade
Ranting alone, skulking the fates of man.
I cast him also, and a third began
And he too died. But I am none of those.
Is there another still to die . . . Who knows?"

25

Then in his pain, half wondering what he did,
He made to struggle towards that belfried place.
And groaning down the sodden bank he slid,
And groaning in the lane he left his trace
Of bloodied mire: then halted with his face
Upwards, towards the gateway, breathing hard
—An old <u>lych-gate</u> before a burial-yard.

Stanza 25

lych-gate: a roofed gateway at
the entrance of a cemetery

26

He looked within. Between the
    huddling crosses,
Over the slanted tombs and sunken slate
Spread the deep quiet grass and humble mosses,
A green and growing darkness, drenched of late,
Smelling of earth and damp. He reached
    the gate
With failing hand. "I will rest here," he said,
"And the long grass will cool my burning head."

CANTO IX

Coming close to despair, Dymer meets an armed sentry, who says he guards against beasts of the upper air and those of the deep sea. He explains that there is a walker-in-the-night, a monster sired by Dymer himself. The angelic watchman understands that Dymer is destined to fight with this beast, and he gives Dymer his armor. A great, pale brute appears, with a ridged back and many eyes. Dymer throws a spear at it, but misses. The angelic watchman hears the battle, but does not see it. He arrives to find Dymer dead amid the flowers. The landscape, which had been as broken and blighted as a battleground, suddenly begins to heal, with the renewal of spring happening all at once, with bright flowers and singing birds. The brute turns into a gleaming god, and all of nature is renewed, as if Balder himself had returned from the dead, and a new golden age had begun.

CANTO IX

1

EVEN as he heard the wicket clash behind
   Came a great wind beneath that seemed
      to tear
The solid graves apart; and deaf and blind
Whirled him upright, like smoke, through
      towering air
Whose levels were as steps of a sky stair.
The parching cold roughened his throat
      with thirst
And pricked him at the heart. This was the first.

2

And as he soared into the next degree,
Suddenly all around him he could hear
Sad strings that fretted inconsolably
And ominous horns that blew both far and near.
There broke his human heart, and his last tear
Froze scalding on his chin. But while
    he heard
He shot like a sped dart into the third.

Stanza 2

NB: "Around" was changed to "round" in *Narrative Poems* (1972).

3

And its first stroke of silence could destroy
The spring of tears forever and compress
From off his lips the curved bow of the boy
Forever. The <u>sidereal</u> loneliness
Received him, where no journeying leaves
    the less
Still to be journeyed through: but everywhere,
Fast though you fly, the centre still is there.

Stanza 3

sidereal: relating to the stars or the expanse between them

4

And here the well-worn fabric of our life
Fell from him. Hope and purpose were
    cut short,
—Even the blind trust that reaches in
    mid-strife
Towards some heart of things. Here blew
    the <u>mort</u>
For the world spirit herself. The last support
Was fallen away—Himself, one spark of soul,
Swam in unbroken void. He was the whole,

Stanza 4

mort: In hunting, the sound of the horn announcing the death of the hunted animal.

5

And wailing: "Why hast Thou forsaken me?
Was there no world at all, but only I
Dreaming of gods and men?" Then suddenly
He felt the wind no more: he seemed to fly
Faster than light but free, and scaled the sky
In his own strength—as if a falling stone
Should wake to find the world's will was
                                its own.

6

And on the instant, straight before his eyes
He looked and saw a sentry shape that stood
Leaning upon its spear, with hurrying skies
Behind it and a moonset red as blood.
Upon its head were helmet and mailed hood,
And shield upon its arm and sword at thigh,
All black and pointed sharp against the sky.

7

Then came the clink of metal, the dry sound
Of steel on rock, and challenge: "Who
                                comes here?"
And as he heard it, Dymer at one bound
Stood in the stranger's shadow, with the spear
Between them. And his human face came near
That larger face. "What watch is this you keep,"
Said Dymer, "on the edge of such a deep?"

8

And answer came, "I watch both night and day
This frontier . . . there are beasts of the upper air

As beasts of the deep sea . . . one walks this way
Night after night, far scouring from his lair,
Chewing the cud of lusts which are despair
And fill not, while his mouth gapes dry
     for bliss
That never was."—"What kind of beast is this?"

9

"A kind of things escaped that have no home,
Hunters of men. They love the spring uncurled,
The will worn down, the wearied hour.
     They come
At night-time when the mask is off the world
And the soul's gate ill-locked and the
     flag furled
—Then, softly, a pale swarm, and in disguise,
Flit past the drowsy watchman, small as flies."

10

—"I'll see this aerish beast whereof you speak.
I'll share the watch with you."—"Nay, little One,
Begone. You are of earth. The flesh is weak. . . ."
—"What is the flesh to me? My course is run,
All but some deed still waiting to be done,
Some moment I may rise on, as the boat
Lifts with the lifting tide and steals afloat.

Stanza 10

"The flesh is weak": Matthew
26:41, "The spirit is willing, but
the flesh is weak."

11

"You are a spirit, and it is well with you,
But I am come out of great folly and shame,
The sack of cities, wrongs I must undo. . . .
But tell me of the beast, and whence it came;

Who were its sire and dam? What is its name?"
—"It is my kin. All monsters are the brood
Of heaven and earth, and mixed with
            holy blood."

12

—"How can this be?"—"My son, sit
            here awhile.

Stanza 12

sons of heaven: A possible
allusion to Genesis 6:1-4, where
the sons of heaven mate with
the daughters of earth.

There is a lady in that primal place
Where I was born, who with her ancient smile
Made glad the <u>sons of heaven</u>. She loved to
            chase
The springtime round the world. To all
            your race
She was a sudden quivering in the wood
Or a new thought springing in solitude.

13

"Till, in prodigious hour, one swollen
            with youth,
Blind from new-broken prison, knowing not
Himself nor her, nor how to mate with truth,
Lay with her in a strange and secret spot,
Mortal with her immortal, and begot
This walker-in-the-night"—"But did you know
This mortal's name?"—"Why . . . it was
            long ago.

14

"And yet, I think, I bear the name in mind;
It was some famished boy whom
            tampering men

Had crippled in their chains and made
        him blind
Till their weak hour discovered them: and then
He broke that prison. Softly!—it comes again,
I have it. It was Dymer, little One,
Dymer's the name. This spectre is his son."

15

Then, after silence, came an answering shout
From Dymer, glad and full: "Break off! Dismiss!
Your watch is ended and your lamp is out.
Unarm, unarm. Return into your bliss.
You are relieved, Sir. I must deal with this
As in my right. For either I must slay
This beast or else be slain before the day."

16

"So mortal and so brave?" that other said,
  Smiling, and turned and looked in
      Dymer's eyes,
Scanning him over twice from heel to head
—Like an old sergeant's glance, grown
      battle-wise
To know the points of men. At last, "Arise,"
He said, "and wear my arms. I can withhold
Nothing; for such an hour has been foretold."

17

Thereat, with lips as cold as the sea-surge,
He kissed the youth, and bending on one knee
Put all his armour off and let emerge
Angelic shoulders marbled gloriously

And feet like frozen speed and, plain to see,
On his wide breast dark wounds and
              ancient scars,
The battle honours of celestial wars.

18

Then like a squire or brother born he dressed
The young man in those plates, that dripped
              with cold
Upon the inside, trickling over breast
And shoulder: but without, the figured gold
Gave to the tinkling ice its jagged hold,
And the icy spear froze fast to Dymer's hand.
But where the other had stood he took
              his stand

19

And searched the cloudy landscape. He
              could see
Dim shapes like hills appearing, but the moon
Had sunk behind their backs. "When will it be?"
Said Dymer: and the other, "Soon now, soon.
For either he comes past us at night's noon
Or else between the night and the full day,
And down there, on your left, will be his way."

20

—"Swear that you will not come between us two
Nor help me by a hair's weight if I bow."
—"If you are he, if prophecies speak true,
Not heaven and all the gods can help you now.
This much I have been told, but know not how

The fight will end. Who knows? I cannot tell."
"Sir, be content," said Dymer. "I know well."

21

Thus Dymer stood to arms, with eyes
    that ranged
Through aching darkness: stared upon it, so
That all things, as he looked upon them,
    changed
And were not as at first. But grave and slow
The larger shade went sauntering to and fro,
Humming at first the snatches of some tune
That soldiers sing, but falling silent soon.

22

Then came steps of dawn. And though
    they heard
No milking cry in the fields, and no cock crew,
And out of empty air no twittering bird
Sounded from neighbouring hedges, yet
    they knew.
Eastward the hollow blackness paled to blue,
Then blue to white: and in the West the rare,
Surviving stars blinked feebler in cold air.

23

Far beneath Dymer's feet the sad half-light
Discovering the new landscape oddly came,
And forms grown half familiar in the night
Looked strange again: no distance seemed
    the same.
And now he could see clear and call by name

Stanza 23

NB: "Far" was changed to "For" in *Narrative Poems* (1972).

Valleys and hills and woods. The phantoms all
Took shape, and made a world, at
            morning's call.

24

It was a <u>ruinous land</u>. The ragged stumps
Of broken trees rose out of endless clay
Naked of flower and grass: the slobbered humps
Dividing the dead pools. Against the grey
A shattered village gaped. But now the day
Was very near them and the night was past,
And Dymer understood and spoke at last.

25

"Now I have wooed and won you, bridal earth,
Beautiful world that lives, desire of men.
All that the spirit intended at my birth
This day shall be born into deed . . . and then
The hard day's labour comes no more again
Forever. The pain dies. The longings cease.
The ship glides under the green arch of peace.

26

"Now drink me as the sun drinks up the mist.
This is the hour to cease in, at full flood,
That asks no gift from following years—but, hist!
Look yonder! At the corner of that wood—
Look! Look there where he comes! It shocks
            the blood,
The first sight, eh? Now, sentinel, stand clear
And save yourself. For God's sake come
            not near."

27

His full-grown spirit had moved without
    command
Or spur of the will. Before he knew, he found
That he was leaping forward spear in hand
To where that ashen brute wheeled
    slowly round
Nosing, and set its ears towards the sound,
The pale and heavy brute, rough-ridged behind,
And full of eyes, clinking in scaly rind.

28

And now ten paces parted them: and here
He halted. He thrust forward his left foot,
Poising his straightened arms, and launched
    the spear,
And gloriously it sang. But now the brute
Lurched forward: and he saw the weapon shoot
Beyond it and fall quivering on the field.
Dymer drew out his sword and raised
    the shield.

29

What now, my friends? You get no more
    from me
Of Dymer. He goes from us. What he felt
Or saw from henceforth no man knows but he
Who has himself gone through the jungle belt
Of dying, into peace. That angel knelt
Far off and watched them close but could
    not see
Their battle. All was ended suddenly.

Stanza 29

NB: Comma between "now"
and "my" was omitted in
Narrative Poems (1972).

30

A leap—a cry—flurry of steel and claw,
Then silence. As before, the morning light
And the same brute crouched yonder; and
      he saw
Under its feet, broken and bent and white,
The ruined limbs of Dymer, killed outright
All in a moment, all his story done.
  . . . But that same moment came the rising sun;

31

And thirty miles to westward, the grey cloud
Flushed into answering pink.
      Long shadows streamed
From every hill, and the low-hanging shroud
Of mist along the valleys broke and steamed
Gold-flecked to heaven. Far off the
      armour gleamed
Like glass upon the dead man's back. But now
The sentinel ran forward, hand to brow,

Stanza 32

The rejuvenation of the earth after Dymer's death suggests that he is a kind of "corn god," a dying god whose death brings about new life on earth. Lewis would later consider the dying god myth to be an important argument for the "true myth" of Christianity, the death and resurrection of Christ. Also, a similar rapid onset of spring and regeneration anticipates the coming of Aslan to Narnia in *The Lion, the Witch and the Wardrobe*.

32

And staring. For between him and the sun
He saw that country clothed with
      dancing flowers
Where flower had never grown; and one by one
The splintered woods, as if from April showers,
Were softening into green. In the leafy towers
Rose the cool, sudden chattering on
      the tongues
Of happy birds with morning in their lungs.

33

The wave of flowers came breaking round
    his feet,
Crocus and bluebell, primrose, daffodil
Shivering with moisture: and the air grew sweet
Within his nostrils, changing heart and will,
Making him laugh. He looked, and Dymer still
Lay dead among the flowers and
    pinned beneath
The brute: but as he looked he held his breath;

34

For when he had gazed hard with steady eyes
Upon the brute, behold, no brute was there,
But someone towering large against the skies,
*A wing'd and sworded shape, whose
    foam-like hair
Lay white about its shoulders, and the air
That came from it was burning hot. The whole
Pure body brimmed with life, as a full bowl.

35

And from the distant corner of day's birth
He heard clear trumpets blowing and bells ring,
A noise of great good coming into earth
And such a music as the dumb would sing
If Balder had led back the blameless spring
With victory, with the voice of charging spears,
And in white lands long-lost Saturnian years.

THE END

Stanza 35

A noise of great good coming: Compare to the last paragraph of George MacDonald's novel *Phantastes*: "A great good is coming—is coming, is coming." Lewis first read this story when he was seventeen years old. It had a profound impact on Lewis's own spiritual journey and his eventual conversion to Christianity.

Balder: In Norse mythology, a beautiful god killed by the blind giant Hod at the instigation of Loki. In his memoir *Surprised by Joy* (1955), Lewis recalls that one of his earliest experiences of "Joy," longing for the unattainable, was when he read the words in Longfellow:
    I heard a voice that cried,
    Balder the beautiful
    Is dead, is dead—
Balder would become one example of the dying god myth that so fascinated Lewis. He incorporated the idea into the ending of *Dymer*, and he later identified Christ as the dying God who significantly was an historical figure, not just a mythological character.

Saturnian years: In classical mythology, a golden age.

APPENDIX

Table 1. Differences introduced by the first American edition (E. P. Dutton, 1926). First Edition/1926 British (J. M. Dent) and 1950 British reprint (J. M. Dent) are identical apart from revisions to Canto IX, Stanza 34 (noted below).

Canto. Stanza	First Edition/1926 British (J. M. Dent) and 1950 British edition (J. M. Dent)	First American edition 1926 (E. P. Dutton), variant text introduced
1.3	the State,	the State
1.4	masterly	mastery
1.5	spring-time	spring time
1.10	unbelieving awe.	unbelieving awe,
1.10	finger-tips,	finger tips,
1.11	sun-stream	sum-stream
1.11	high-hanging lark,	high hanging lark
1.11	behind him,	behind him.
1.13	and North,	and North
1.15	and white,	and white
1.16	long enough;	long enough,
1.19	of a wood,	of a wood
1.19	swimming red,	swimming red
1.21	a place:	a place.
1.22	hat-stand	hatstand
1.28	white-flowered	white flowered
1.29	so bless,	so bless
1.29	the ceiling,	the ceiling.
1.29	peacefulness,	peacefulness
1.31	bolted door;	bolted door,
1.32	Someone's here.	Someone's here,
2.2	perspective, till	perspective till
2.5	wild-eyed	wild eyed
2.13	prawns	prauns
2.21	O God, the pity	Oh God, the pity
2.22	O splendour	Oh splendour
2.22	O world arrayed	oh world arrayed

Canto. Stanza	First Edition/1926 British (J. M. Dent) and 1950 British edition (J. M. Dent)	First American edition 1926 (E. P. Dutton), variant text introduced
2.28	thunder-showers	thundershowers
2.29	roughly sweet,	roughly sweet
2.32	seven-league	seven league
3.2	loose-limbed	loose limbed
3.2	drowsy-eyed	drowsy eyed
3.4	sighed anew;	sighed anew:
3.7	young leaves, where	young leaves where
3.14	Shaking himself, he ran	Shaking himself he ran
3.15	to the sky,	to the sky
3.16	sudden sweat	sudden sweat,
3.18	ended blind,	needed blind,
3.19	, and said:	, and said,
3.23	Immovable	Immoveable
3.28	Old night, put	Old night put
3.29	—so Dymer stood,	So Dymer stood,
3.30	I must go in."	I must go in.
3.31	from your law;	from your law
4.2	He stooped,	He stooped
4.3	Light was none,	Light was none
4.10	Of work-day	Of work day
4.11	weary to death,	weary to death
4.12	Damn you!	Damn you.
4.12	O my God!	oh my God!
4.13	Listen: I've	Listen, I've
4.16	one day, one man	one day one man
4.17	I cannot say—	I cannot say,
4.19	word spoken)	word spoken),
4.21	'Dymer!' they cried.	'Dymer' they cried.
4.23	were coarse,	were coarse
4.27	'Die, then!'	'Die, then'
4.27	'That's for you!'	'That's for you.'
4.28	shattered skull,	shattered skull
4.33	have thought—	have thought,
4.34	my blood.	my blood
4.35	East	east

Canto. Stanza	First Edition/1926 British (J. M. Dent) and 1950 British edition (J. M. Dent)	First American edition 1926 (E. P. Dutton), variant text introduced
5.3	world-despair	world despair
5.7	rose upright,	rose upright
5.8	old stone:	old stone,
5.14	built	build
5.14	Nature	nature
5.16	nations slept	nations slept,
5.16	the light;	the light,
5.20	they burn,	they burn
5.21	wreaths	wreathes
5.24	said he; "not yet."	said he. "Not yet."
5.26	he slept,	he slept
5.26	trembled through,	trembled through
5.30	was but a bird's	was a bird's
5.32	foothills	foot hills
6.4	in the sky, and	in the sky and
6.10	"What, Sir!" said	"What, Sir," said
6.13	and the floor	and the floor,
6.17	O my soul,	Oh my soul,
6.21	shall forget),	shall forget)
6.23	gods	Gods
6.26	good words go?—	good words go?
6.30	among men?	among men!
6.31	or once again,	or once again
6.33	counted	counting
6.36	"never	"Never
6.36	Oh, lies, all lies	Oh lies, all lies
7.2	hedgerows	hedgegrows
7.4	finger-tip,	finger tip,
7.6	for the asking!	for the asking.
7.8	Theomagia	Theogmagia
7.8	grubs	grules
7.9	one and all,	one and all
7.9	sickening	sickened
7.12	Bogies	Bogys
7.17	deer at play,	deer at play

Canto. Stanza	First Edition/1926 British (J. M. Dent) and 1950 British edition (J. M. Dent)	First American edition 1926 (E. P. Dutton), variant text introduced
7.17	Oh, sweet!	Oh sweet!
7.22	Hesperian	Hesperean
7.22	one far, spent	one farspent
7.28	devil-dancers'	devil dancers
7.28	swamp,	swamp
7.30	Crooning,	Crooning
7.31	Begone!"—"With	Begone."—"With
7.32	levelled gun,	levelled gun
8.3	the heavens:	the heavens;
8.5	it was strange:	it was strange;
8.6	—"Oh, lady,	"Oh, lady,
8.11	gods themselves, that	gods themselves that
8.14	"What!"	"What,"
8.15	Our beauty can	Our beauty, can
8.19	Go forth;	Go forth,
8.22	thought—"like this,	thought. "Like this,
8.22	or worse,	or worse
8.23	Reign	Reigns
8.25	he slid,	he slid
8.25	left his trace	felt his trace
9.1	upright, like smoke,	upright like smoke,
9.1	towering air	towering air.
9.4	of our life	of our life,
9.5	but free,	but free;
9.6	mailed hood,	mailed hood
9.7	keep?"	keep,"
9.7	deep."	deep?"
9.7	"on the edge	"On the edge
9.9	in disguise,	in disguise
9.10	—"I'll see this	"I'll see this
9.13	new-broken	new broken
9.14	little One,	Little One,
9.20	prophecies	prophesies
9.27	he knew, he	he knew he
9.31	westward	Westward

Canto. Stanza	First Edition/1926 British (J. M. Dent) and 1950 British edition (J. M. Dent)	First American edition 1926 (E. P. Dutton), variant text introduced
9.31	low-hanging	low hanging
*9.34	[1950 British printed in text]	*see below

FIRST EDITION (CANTO IX, STANZA 34)

*A wing'd and sworded shape, through whom the air
Poured as through glass: and its foam-tumbled hair
Lay white about the shoulders and the whole
Pure body brimmed with life, as a full bowl.

Table 2. Variant text introduced in *Narrative Poems* (1972)

Canto. Stanza	First Edition/1926 British and 1950 British edition	Narrative Poems (1972)
2.32	seven-league	seven-leagued
3.4	wheeling	wheeled
3.13	Breasts	Breast
4.3	rain-steam	rain-stream
4.20	lying wide awake	lying awake
5.19	gulley's	gully's
9.2	around him	round him
9.7	"on the edge	'on edge
9.23	Far beneath	For beneath
9.29	What now, my friends	What now my friends

HANSEN LECTURES

Jerry Root

INTRODUCTION

Walter Hansen

I HAD NOT READ *Dymer* until Jerry Root announced his plan to deliver these lectures. My first reading was slow going as I struggled to follow Dymer on his strange journey told in the archaic, intricate rhyme royal structure of this narrative poem. As I pushed myself forward through the poem, trying to grasp some meaning, I wondered why the poem was so opaque. Why didn't it have the exceptional clarity I enjoyed in all the other books by Lewis?

However, after listening to Jerry's illuminating lectures, I was delighted in my second reading to see some fascinating connections between this poem and my favorite books by Lewis. Because Jerry has comprehensive knowledge of all that Lewis wrote, he is able to show that this poem, written five years before Lewis was converted to Christianity, contains many seeds that blossom in his later works. After reading Jerry's lectures and the responses to him, I followed Dymer a third time and realized with amazement how much his journey of self-discovery mirrors the journey of Lewis as a young atheist longing for meaning and fulfillment in his life.

Dymer's journey strips him of seductive and destructive illusions: political revolutions; illicit, impersonal sexual pleasures; dreams induced by hallucinatory drugs; and occult powers—to name a few illusions that Dymer pursued and then fled when they proved false. Lewis vividly portrays the power of these illusions. The reader cannot help but be tempted to fall under their spell. But Lewis also presents the horror of the consequences: pursuing these illusions leads to alienation, loneliness, violence, and death. Reading the poem not only shows me how disillusioned Lewis became in his own journey through life, but also awakens me to the power of illusions and their consequences in my own world. The poem strengthens my resolve to pursue reality, not illusions.

Dymer's journey closes the way to one option after another. When he tries to go back into the palace to find the unknown girl who seduced him the night before, a dreadful old hag blocks every door. Lost in the woods, "against him even the clouds and winds conspire." Mesmerized in a dream world after drinking from the cup of the Magician, he awakes thirsting for reality. Finally, facing a monster, he chooses death as the only way out. His entire journey led him from one bitter loss to another.

Early in the poem we get a glimpse of Dymer's miserable condition:

See Dymer with drooped head and knocking knees
Comes from the porch. Then slowly, drunkly reeling,
Blind, beaten, broken, past desire of healing,
Past knowledge of his misery, he goes on
Under the first dark trees and now is gone.
(III.33)

Dymer never reached what Lewis experienced as "checkmate."[1] Every move Lewis made to escape "the steady, unrelenting approach of Him I so earnestly desired not to meet"[2] was checked and blocked. Doors slammed shut. Walls barred the way forward. Lewis was finally left with no other option except to kneel and admit that God was God, "perhaps, that night, the most dejected and reluctant convert in all England."[3] After I read *Dymer*, I gave thanks to God for checkmating Lewis, closing all options to him, and finally leading him to total surrender to God.

The poem not only relates how Dymer's journey destroys his illusions and thwarts his egocentric plans, but also portrays Dymer in times of

---

[1]C. S. Lewis, *Surprised by Joy* (New York: Harcourt, Brace and Company, 1955), 212.
[2]Lewis, *Surprised by Joy*, 228.
[3]Lewis, *Surprised by Joy*, 228-29.

ecstasy "wondering like a child" (II.5), drinking until "Rapture flew / Through every vein" (II.18), crushing "wet, cool flowers against his face" (I.17), hearing "the music, unendurable / In stealing sweetness wind from tree to tree" (I.27), putting on royal clothes, "bright as blood and clear as morning skies" (II.6), awakening to the "pure voice of a lark that seemed to send / Its song from heights beyond all height" (V.27)—these and other experiences of transcendent beauty make Dymer long for more. But Dymer never found fulfillment of his inconsolable longing. His journey ended when a monster killed him.

After Dymer's death, a sentinel saw that

> The wave of flowers came breaking round his feet,
> Crocus and bluebell, primrose, daffodil
> Shivering with moisture: and the air grew sweet
> Within his nostrils, changing heart and will,
> Making him laugh. He looked, and Dymer still
> Lay dead among the flowers
> (IX.33)

The end of the poem gives a vivid image of the new birth of spring:

> And from the distant corner of day's birth
> He heard clear trumpets blowing and bells ring,
> A noise of great good coming into earth
> And such a music as the dumb would sing
> If Balder had led back the blameless spring
> With victory, with the voice of charging spears,
> And in white lands long-lost Saturnian years.
> (IX.35)

This conclusion of *Dymer* draws from the Norse mythology of Balder, the son of Odin. Lewis first learned this myth as a boy when he idly turned the pages of his father's book of Henry Wadsworth Longfellow's poems and found the death dirge poem "Tegner's Drapa."

I heard the voice that cried
Balder the Beautiful
Is dead, is dead-[4]

The myth turns from the death of Balder to a new birth of life:

But out of the sea of Time
Rises a new land of song,
Fairer than the old.
Over its meadows green
Walk the young bards and sing."

Lewis described his childhood response to his first reading of this myth: "I knew nothing about Balder; but instantly I was uplifted into huge regions of northern sky, I desired with almost sickening intensity something never to be described (except that it is cold, spacious, severe, and remote) and then, as in the other examples, found myself at the very same moment already falling out of that desire and wishing I were back in it."[5] The myth of the death of Balder cast an enchanting spell on the young Lewis and inspired him even as a disillusioned atheist to express his hope for a "blameless spring" in the last lines of *Dymer*.

Years later, on a long night walk in Oxford, J. R. R. Tolkien, his colleague at Oxford and fellow lover of Norse mythology, helped Lewis to embrace the gospel story of Jesus as the true fulfillment in history of the old myths of dying and rising gods. C. S. Lewis surrendered his life to God, and throughout the rest of his life he served the crucified and risen Lord Jesus by voluminous writing as a leading apologist of the Christian faith. A result of his conversion can be seen by comparing his view of a "blameless spring" based merely on the myth of Balder and his view of the rebirth of spring based on his belief in the fulfillment of that myth in the gospel of Jesus. In one of his most popular stories, *The Lion, the Witch and the Wardrobe*, Aslan came to the world he created, by his redemptive death turned the

[4]Lewis, *Surprised by Joy*, 17.
[5]Lewis, *Surprised by Joy*, 17.

barren, endless winter into the flourishing beauty of spring, and restored life to his creatures frozen in stone.

As a poem written years before Lewis came to Christian faith, *Dymer* shows me how an atheist is stripped of his false illusions and blocked by one obstacle after another as he stumbles on his way to self-destruction. It also enchants me with images of haunting beauty and glimmers of shimmering hope. Above all, the poem fills my heart with praise that God's love led Lewis beyond the journey of the disillusioned Dymer, mercifully drew him to believe that Jesus Christ is the Son of God, and uniquely granted him the gift of writing with such exceptional clarity so that many have come to faith in Christ through his books.

I could not have deciphered the obscure meaning of *Dymer* without the wise guidance of Jerry Root. As he leads you in these lectures, I hope that you will read *Dymer* with great pleasure and be amazed to see how themes in this poem are fully developed in the greatly loved stories and essays that C. S. Lewis wrote to teach us that "the Christian story is precisely the story of one grand miracle . . . what is uncreated, eternal, came into nature, into human nature, descended into His own universe, and rose again, bringing up nature with Him."[6]

THE KEN AND JEAN HANSEN LECTURESHIP

I was motivated to set up a lectureship in honor of my parents, Ken and Jean Hansen, at the Wade Center primarily because they loved Marion E. Wade. My father began working for Mr. Wade in 1946, the year I was born. He launched my father's career and mentored him in business. Often when I look at the picture of Marion Wade in the Wade Center, I give thanks to God for his beneficial influence in my family and in my life.

After Darlene and I were married in December 1967, the middle of my senior year at Wheaton College, we invited Marion and Lil Wade for dinner in our apartment. I wanted Darlene to get to know the best storyteller I've ever heard.

[6]C. S. Lewis, "The Grand Miracle" in *God in the Dock* (Grand Rapids, MI: Eerdmans, 1970), 80.

When Marion Wade passed through death into the Lord's presence on November 28, 1973, his last words to my father were, "Remember Joshua, Ken." As Joshua was the one who followed Moses to lead God's people, my father was the one who followed Marion Wade to lead the Service-Master Company.

After members of Marion Wade's family and friends at ServiceMaster set up a memorial fund in honor of Marion Wade at Wheaton College, my parents initiated the renaming of Clyde Kilby's collection of papers and books from the seven British authors—C. S. Lewis, J. R. R. Tolkien, Dorothy L. Sayers, George MacDonald, G. K. Chesterton, Charles Williams, and Owen Barfield—as the Marion E. Wade Collection.

I'm also motivated to name this lectureship after my parents because they loved the literature of these seven authors whose papers are now collected at the Wade Center.

While I was still in college, my father and mother took an evening course on Lewis and Tolkien with Dr. Kilby. The class was limited to nine students so that they could meet in Dr. Kilby's living room. Dr. Kilby's wife, Martha, served tea and cookies.

My parents were avid readers, collectors, and promoters of the books of the seven Wade authors, even hosting a book club in their living room led by Dr. Kilby. When they moved to Santa Barbara in 1977, they named their home Rivendell, after the beautiful house of the elf Lord Elrond, whose home served as a welcome haven to weary travelers as well as a cultural center for Middle-earth history and lore. Family and friends who stayed in their home know that their home fulfilled Tolkien's description of Rivendell:

> And so at last they all came to the Last Homely House, and found
> its doors flung wide. . . . [The] house was perfect whether you liked
> food, or sleep, or work, or story-telling, or singing, or just sitting and
> thinking best, or a pleasant mixture of them all. . . . Their clothes

were mended as well as their bruises, their tempers and their hopes. . . . Their plans were improved with the best advice.[7]

Our family treasures many memories of our times at Rivendell, highlighted by storytelling. Our conversations often drew from images of the stories of Lewis, Tolkien, and the other authors. We had our own code language: "That was a terrible Bridge of Khazad-dûm experience." "That meeting felt like the Council of Elrond."

One cold February, Clyde and Martha Kilby escaped the deep freeze of Wheaton to thaw out and recover for two weeks at my parents' Rivendell home in Santa Barbara. As a thank-you note, Clyde Kilby dedicated his book *Images of Salvation in the Fiction of C. S. Lewis* to my parents. When my parents set up our family foundation in 1985, they named the foundation Rivendell Stewards' Trust.

In many ways, they lived in and lived out the stories of the seven authors. It seems fitting and proper, therefore, to name this lectureship in honor of Ken and Jean Hansen.

ESCAPE FOR PRISONERS

The purpose of the Hansen Lectureship is to provide a way of escape for prisoners. J. R. R. Tolkien writes about the positive role of escape in literature:

I have claimed that Escape is one of the main functions of fairy-stories, and since I do not disapprove of them, it is plain that I do not accept the tone of scorn or pity with which "Escape" is now so often used: a tone for which the uses of the word outside literary criticism give no warrant at all. In what the misusers of Escape are fond of calling Real Life, Escape is evidently as a rule very practical, and may even be heroic.[8]

---

[7] J. R. R. Tolkien, *The Hobbit* (London: Unwin Hyman, 1987), 50-51.
[8] J. R. R. Tolkien, "On Fairy-Stories," in *Tales from the Perilous Realm* (Boston: Houghton Mifflin, 2008), 375.

Note that Tolkien is not talking about escap*ism* or an avoidance of reality but rather the idea of escape as a means of providing a new view of reality, the true, transcendent reality that is often screened from our view in this fallen world. He adds:

> Evidently we are faced by a misuse of words, and also by a con-fusion of thought. Why should a man be scorned, if, finding himself in prison, he tries to get out and go home? Or if, when he cannot do so, he thinks and talks about other topics than jailers and prison-walls? The world outside has not become less real be-cause the prisoner cannot see it. In using Escape in this [derog-atory] way the [literary] critics have chosen the wrong word, and, what is more, they are confusing, not always by sincere error, the Escape of the Prisoner with the Flight of the Deserter.[9]

I am not proposing that these lectures give us a way to escape from our responsibilities or ignore the needs of the world around us but rather that we explore the stories of the seven authors to escape from a distorted view of reality, from a sense of hopelessness, and to awaken us to the true hope of what God desires for us and promises to do for us.

C. S. Lewis offers a similar vision for the possibility that such literature could open our eyes to a new reality:

> We want to escape the illusions of perspective. . . . We want to see with other eyes, to imagine with other imaginations, to feel with other hearts, as well as with our own. . . .
>
> The man who is contented to be only himself, and therefore less a self, is in prison. My own eyes are not enough for me, I will see through those of others. . . .
>
> In reading great literature I become a thousand men yet remain myself. . . . Here as in worship, in love, in moral action, and in

---

[9]Tolkien, "On Fairy-Stories," 376.

knowing, I transcend myself; and am never more myself than when I do.[10]

The purpose of the Hansen Lectureship is to explore the great literature of the seven Wade authors so that we can escape from the prison of our self-centeredness and narrow, parochial perspective in order to see with other eyes, feel with other hearts, and be equipped for practical deeds in real life.

As a result, we will learn new ways to experience and extend the fulfillment of our Lord's mission: "to proclaim freedom for the prisoners and recovery of sight for the blind, to set the oppressed free" (Lk 4:18 NIV).

---

[10]C. S. Lewis, *An Experiment in Criticism* (Cambridge: Cambridge University, 1965), 137, 140-41.

1

"A SPLENDOUR IN THE DARK, A TALE, A SONG"

BEFORE *DYMER* IS ANYTHING, it is a story C. S. Lewis longed to tell. He said it "arrived, complete, in my mind somewhere about my seventeenth year."[1] From the time it was conceived until publication, eleven years passed, as the story percolated in his mind and heart. It was "A splendour in the dark, a tale, a song."[2] However, for most, *Dymer* is a little-known narrative poem written by Lewis before he became a Christian. Consequently, those only interested in Lewis's postconversion perspective often overlook it. Nevertheless, to understand Lewis as a multifaceted writer, *Dymer* remains significant, and those wanting to do serious Lewis study must not overlook the riches to be mined from this book.

I intend to show that *Dymer* is an important work, even though often neglected. In fact, many do not even know of its existence. It is the longest and most developed of his narrative poems. Consequently, it reveals best the kind of work Lewis was doing when he dreamed of becoming a poet. Furthermore, *Dymer* has, in seed, several big ideas that would come to full fruit in his mature work. Therefore, the poem could be considered a preview of what was to come in his later imaginative fiction. It must also be added that while Lewis's vocational dream to be a poet would never

---

[1]C. S. Lewis, *Dymer: Wade Annotated Edition* in Jerry Root, *Splendour in the Dark: C. S. Lewis's* Dymer *in His Life and Work* (Downers Grove, IL: IVP Academic 2020), 9. Cf. C. S. Lewis, *Dymer* (London: J. M. Dent & Sons LTD, 1950), ix.

[2]*Dymer*, V.29.

become a reality, the disciplined and economical use of words so characteristic of Lewis's writing are originally on public display in this text.

REALITY IS ICONOCLASTIC

The poet Lewis was preoccupied with disappointments and dashed hopes. Things seldom happened as expected. His mother died when he was only nine. He was born with a deformity of his thumbs that made him awkward; consequently, at school games he was the subject of derision. He grew pessimistic. In his first meeting with his tutor, William T. Kirkpatrick, he was chided for having a preconceived notion of what Surrey, England, was like (a place Lewis had never seen until then). Add to this his war experiences, and it is not surprising to discover that Lewis would engage his imagination in developing a story where the primary character wrestles with a sense of not belonging and a preoccupation to find his place and try to fit in. To the degree anyone might struggle with such things, Dymer, the character of the poem, becomes an everyman; and through this character, Lewis begins to explore imaginatively one of his biggest themes, that *reality is iconoclastic*. An iconoclast breaks idols. An imaginative grasp of any topic, held too tightly, becomes unresponsive to development. In such cases, the image can calcify and become brittle. When this occurs, it becomes something like an idol, thereby truncating development and growth. I seek to demonstrate that Lewis uses *Dymer* as a means to wrestle with this idea.

Furthermore, Lewis wrote, "We do not enjoy a story fully at the first reading. Not till the curiosity, the sheer narrative lust has been given its sop and laid to sleep, are we at leisure to enjoy the real beauties. Till then, it is like wasting great wine on a ravenous natural thirst which merely wants cold wetness."[3] This first of three chapters familiarizes the reader with the "narrative sop" and explores the big theme Lewis is imaginatively developing around his central character.

---

[3]C. S. Lewis, *Of Other Worlds: Essays and Stories*, ed. Walter Hooper (New York: Harcourt, Brace & World, 1966), 18.

WITH ALL MY ROAD BEFORE ME

"With all my road before me"—these words come from the first verse of the first canto of *Dymer*. The signal and clarion call is clear. The main character—Dymer—is at the beginning of an adventure full of high hopes and aspiration. Readers may naturally wonder where they are likely to be taken. Imaginatively speaking, Dymer's story becomes their story. The language is evocative of adventures, which lie ahead for the protagonist. Dymer is young, naïve, and full of ambition. He is full of hopes and expectations. The unexpected bruisings are yet to come.

Could the words "With all my road before me" also reveal the author's own enthusiasm for the prospects before him as he wondered where the publication of this book might lead? Perhaps, but probably not. Lewis, at the end of the next decade, would write that we do not study an author's books to discover the author. In fact, he argued that we look through the author's eyes, but not at him. We see what he sees. We use the author as spectacles; we do not make a spectacle of him or her. Some may suggest that the practice of trying to identify an author's autobiographical features within his book is a violation of literary criticism, a demonstration of what Lewis called "the personal heresy."[4] In reality, Lewis warns critics against trying to analyze the author who is not present, meanwhile avoiding the very text before them. Such a practice in criticism would be analogous to the informal fallacy known as a "red herring," that is, to become distracted from the task at hand in order to chase after something that is, to the point, irrelevant. Nevertheless, it would be shortsighted to suggest that the author never uses anything from his own experience to tell a story. In fact, Lewis writes of "the shared imagination" as the creative asset that draws on one's personal experience in a way that allows connection with the "shared experience" of others. Consequently, a deeper connection can occur imaginatively between author and reader to the degree that they recognize a connecting link between them.

---

[4]C. S. Lewis and E. M. W. Tillyard, *The Personal Heresy* (London: Oxford, 1939).

So too, in this story, Lewis intends to draw his readers into the narrative. He rightly knows that virtually all who have set out on adventures tend to come to them with excitement and wonder, perhaps even with a measure of fear of the unknown. He uses what he knows of himself, others, and life in general to bond as one: author, reader, and story. Furthermore, one can almost feel Lewis's excitement as he is on the threshold of his literary career. He still has the hopes that he might one day emerge as a great poet. Those dreams had not yet crashed for him into disappointment. The reader knows that Lewis would achieve great success as a writer, but it would not come about as a poet. Nevertheless, *Dymer* still contains themes, in seed, that suggest the fruit of things to come. The book met with some positive reviews and almost no sales; nonetheless, it remains significant for all who want to understand Lewis's development as an author.

WHY IS *DYMER* SO IMPORTANT?

Given its place at the beginning of the Lewis corpus, *Dymer* is important in the same way that an acorn is important to the oak. *Dymer* being Lewis's only full-length narrative poem makes it a literary artifact most robustly representing his early career as a poet. The lengthy poem was published in book form five years before he became a Christian. Apart from his journal and his early letters, *Dymer* is the longest work available to readers that captures his sustained, pre-Christian voice. Why is this important?

Lewis acknowledged early in his academic career that "Humanity does not pass through phases as a train passes through stations: being alive, it has the privilege of always moving yet never leaving anything behind. Whatever we have been, in some sort we are still."[5] Toward the end of his life, he still believes this and writes, "The process of growing up is to be valued for what we gain, not for what we lose."[6] The question is one of continuity. Lewis acknowledged, "Mere change is not growth. Growth is

---

[5]C. S. Lewis, *The Allegory of Love: A Study in Medieval Tradition* (Oxford: Oxford University Press, 1936), 1.

[6]C. S. Lewis, *An Experiment in Criticism* (Cambridge: Cambridge University Press, 1961), 72.

the synthesis of change and continuity, and where there is no continuity there is no growth."[7] He explains further,

> They accuse us of arrested development because we have not lost a taste we had in childhood. But surely arrested development consists not in refusing to lose old things but in failing to add new things. . . . I now enjoy Tolstoy and Jane Austen and Trollope as well as fairy tales and I call that growth: if I had had to lose the fairy tales in order to acquire the novelists, I would not say that I had grown but only that I had changed. A tree grows because it adds rings: a train doesn't grow by leaving one station behind and puffing on to the next.[8]

Lewis acknowledged that what he became after his conversion had continuity with the man he once had been. Consequently, *Dymer* allows a student of Lewis's work to see how the early expressions of his creative imagination allowed him to tease out various ideas throughout a story.

Nevertheless, *Dymer* continues to be overlooked. Perhaps the neglect is because it is a preconversion publication. Perhaps the neglect is due to its being a long narrative poem. It is certainly a work of art, but, unfortunately, the kind of thing seldom read anymore and therefore little discussed. Perhaps for some the neglect is due to its being less accessible than his other works. Whatever the case, I want to show that it is an important book in the Lewis corpus. As Wordsworth wrote that "the child is the father of the man,"[9] it could be said that *Dymer* is the father of Lewisian literature. In other words, *Dymer*, like Lewis's wardrobe door, opens a unique door into the literary imagination of Lewis. How might this be so?

As has been mentioned, Lewis set his heart and mind on becoming a poet. It was his first choice of vocation. He studied great narrative poetry: *Beowulf*, *The Romance of the Rose*, Dante's *Divine Comedy*, the Arthurian

---

[7]C. S. Lewis, "Hamlet: The Prince or the Poem," in *Selected Literary Essays*, ed. Walter Hooper (Cambridge: Cambridge University Press, 1979), 105.

[8]Lewis, *Of Other Worlds*, 25-26.

[9]William Wordsworth, "My Heart Leaps Up When I Behold," in *British Poets of the Nineteenth Century*, ed. Curtis Hidden Page (Boston: Benjamin H. Sanborn, 1904), 26.

lore, Chaucer's *Troilus and Cressida*, Spenser's *The Faerie Queen*, Milton's *Paradise Lost*, and Robert Browning's *The Ring and the Book* were among his favorites. These books inspired him, and he hoped to write in an equally memorable way. Nevertheless, significant recognition was not forthcoming, nor was there much encouragement to continue with the kind of focused energy he poured into *Dymer*. Even so, good came from Lewis's efforts, and it is a good worthy to be studied. What kind of good? Through the practice of a poet, he learned to use words economically; he disciplined himself to be precise. He practiced the art of clarity and mastered the power of depiction. The words he used as a poet mattered and needed to be selected carefully; consequently, his later prose would benefit significantly. He honed his gifts. As a poet, Lewis also learned to write for the ear, increasing his skill at rhythmic cadence and meter. This was also adapted to his prose. It explains why Lewis is so easy to read aloud, and it clarifies why nobody wants to read him hurriedly. However, there is more.

Lewis was a master of using literary form to match what it was he wanted to say. He wrote that when a man writes a love sonnet, he not only loves the beloved, he also loves the sonnet.[10] Similarly, he wrote, "Sometimes Fairy Stories May Say Best What's to be Said."[11] Furthermore, when Lewis chose to write science fiction, his interest was not in depicting technology. He wanted to write Romantic literature to stir up longing in his readers for places that could not be easily situated geographically. The Christian Lewis sought to awaken longing for other worlds. For Lewis a literary classic was a book people desired to read and reread. Perhaps these people return to certain books in much the same way a child after hearing a delightful fairy story exclaims, "Read it again!" Why? Lewis suggests it is because the child desires to return to that world. It speaks to that part of every one of us that longs to go through the looking glass to another realm, or go through a wardrobe door, or travel on the wings of the North Wind, or ride a tornado into Oz. In fact, Lewis suggests it awakens in us a longing

---

[10]C. S. Lewis, *A Preface to Paradise Lost* (London: Oxford University Press, 1942), 3.
[11]Lewis, *Of Other Worlds*, 35-38.

for the only other world we can ever really know, which is Heaven! Lewis used science fiction as a literary form that framed best what he wanted to say. He said a writer selects his form as a sculptor selects his marble.[12] *Dymer* reveals that very early in his literary career, Lewis was already cultivating the practice of selecting a manner to fit his matter, a form to fit his purposes. So, what might this reveal about *Dymer*?

While a narrative poem can be the vehicle for many things, for Lewis it was a form suitable for myth. Myth simply means "story." However, as Lewis used the word *myth*, he had in mind a story that captured something that was "extra-literary"; it works upon the reader "by its particular flavor or quality, rather as a smell or a chord does." Furthermore, "It deals with impossibles and preternaturals," it is "always grave" and "awe-inspiring." "We feel it to be numinous. It is as if some great moment had been communicated to us."[13] Lewis loved to read myth, and he clearly enjoyed creating and telling one. Though Lewis was no more a Christian when he wrote *Dymer* than Virgil was when he wrote *The Aeneid*, nevertheless, both clearly wrote in a way that suggests something of a reality beyond the natural world. In reading the Norse myths, Lewis experienced an awe that escaped him in his childhood.[14] In *Dymer*, Lewis, to some degree, awakens in his reader a sense of the numinous. Both Homer and Virgil used narrative poetry as the vehicle for their myths; Lewis used the same vehicle. The literary form suggests Lewis's deliberate, imaginative intention for the work: to write a myth that allowed him to explore the idea that reality is iconoclastic.

In *A Preface to Paradise Lost* Lewis distinguishes between two types of literary form for communicating myth: primary epic and secondary epic. "Primary epic" is the kind of narrative used by Homer. It is characterized by *objectivity*.[15] That is, the objects described are before the writer's imagination

---

[12]Lewis, *Of Other Worlds*, 36-37.

[13]C. S. Lewis, *An Experiment in Criticism* (Cambridge: Cambridge University Press, 1961), 43-44.

[14]C. S. Lewis, *Surprised by Joy* (New York: Harcourt, Brace and Company, 1956), 77.

[15]C. S. Lewis, *A Preface to Paradise Lost* (London: Oxford University Press, 1954), 23. "The Homeric splendor is the splendor of reality"—that is, the splendor of the objective world.

and set before the reader; nothing is hidden. However, the interior life of the characters *is* hidden, never revealed. It is of little consequence to the telling of the story. The emotions of the characters are in the rear guard of the action.[16] Secondary epic, on the other hand, is used by Virgil in *The Aeneid*. While Lewis is no Virgil, and *Dymer* is no *Aeneid*, nevertheless, Lewis penned his *Dymer* as a kind of "secondary epic" similar to that used by Virgil. A brief explanation, using some of Lewis's own thoughts on the matter, might clarify what he was attempting to do, and in what way his *Dymer* bears at least a faint stylistic echo of the *Aeneid*.

Movement and transformation characterize secondary epic. Aeneas is fleeing Troy, the city of his birth, as the Greeks are sacking it. Similarly, *Dymer* flees his City with its tyrannies. Aeneas leaves behind him the ashes of what once was, but he will never lose the memory. Nevertheless, he is moving toward something that is yet to be, the building of Rome. Lewis observes, "The transformation of the little remnant, the *reliquias*, of the old, into the germ of the new. Hence the sadness of farewells and the alacrity of new beginnings, so conspicuously brought together in the opening of Book III, dominate the whole poem."[17] Virgil's story has both the objective world of the story in view as well as the subjectivity of the characters, which the reader feels deeply. In *Dymer*, Lewis does something similar. Lewis continues,

It is the nature of a vocation to appear to men in the double character of a duty and desire, and Virgil does justice to both. The element of desire is brought out in all those passages where *the Hesperian land* is hinted, prophesied, and "dim-discovered." . . . This is the very portrait of a vocation: a thing that calls or beckons, that calls inexorably, yet you must strain your ears to catch the voice, that insists on being sought, yet refuses to be found.[18]

Furthermore, Lewis notes that Homer "does not really describe anyone's emotions at any particular moment."

[16]Lewis, *A Preface to Paradise Lost* (1954), 29.
[17]Lewis, *A Preface to Paradise Lost* (1954), 35.
[18]Lewis, *A Preface to Paradise Lost* (1954), 36-37

Lewis's Dymer also begins to realize he has such a vocation, and calling. Lewis observes, "To follow the vocation does not mean happiness: but once it has been heard, there is no happiness for those who do not follow."[19]

Lewis, translating Virgil, captures something of the sentiment of *Dymer*.

"Twixt miserable longing for the present land
And far realms that call them by fates' command."[20]

He continues, "It will be seen that in these two lines Virgil, with no intention of allegory, has described once and for all the very quality of most human life as it is experienced by anyone who has not yet risen to holiness or sunk to animality."[21]

In this regard, Lewis notes of Virgil, "He has become almost a great Christian poet. In making his one legend symbolical of the destiny of Rome, he has, willy-nilly, symbolized the destiny of Man."[22] Lewis observes that if one were to develop beyond Virgil, it would be toward religious poetry. In addition, I might add, whether he intended it or not, that is what Lewis has also done in *Dymer*. Those who read it realize that the preconverted Lewis has taken them to the threshold of what is to come; the Christian writer will emerge imminently. This is one more reason why those interested in Lewis should familiarize themselves with this book.

Dymer is a story, and Lewis observes of stories that "To be stories at all they must be series of events: but it must be understood that this series—the plot, as we call it—is only really a net whereby to catch something else. The real theme may be, and perhaps is, something that has no sequence in it, something other than a process and much more like a state or quality."[23] What Lewis does in *Dymer* is to engage the reader in a way that awakens hunger for something beyond the written page. He says, "If the author's plot is only a net, and usually an imperfect

---

[19]Lewis, *A Preface to Paradise Lost* (1954), 37.
[20]Lewis, *A Preface to Paradise Lost* (1954), 37.
[21]Lewis, *A Preface to Paradise Lost* (1954), 38.
[22]Lewis, *A Preface to Paradise Lost* (1954), 38.
[23]Lewis, *Of Other* Worlds, 18.

one, a net of time and event for catching what is not really a process at all, is life much more."[24]

THE NARRATIVE "SOP"

Dymer is a pilgrimage story. The story is rather simple and must be told briefly before analyzing the narrative. Dymer is a young man living in a tyrannical city. While he is being indoctrinated, coerced, and forced to fit into the wishes of his instructors and conditioners, Dymer notices through the window a real spring day. The lines of demarcation contrasting the artificialities of the city and the real world fresh to his senses are too strong. Dymer rises, strikes the lecturer dead, and bolts from the city. He turns from the false to the real. In his quest he comes upon a castle and there, in the dark, he discovers a woman and fornicates with her. In the morning he leaves the castle, but wishing to return, he finds an old hag guarding the door and inhibiting his every attempt to return to the maiden. Dejected, he wanders seeking to find his way. Eventually he happens upon a young man, wounded, blinded, and dying. Dymer seeks to provide comfort, and hears his story. To his shock, the young man curses the name of Dymer. Concealing his own identity, Dymer learns from the man that on the heels of his flight from the city an insurgent named Bran led a rebellion and many revolted with him. Bran, nevertheless, in dictator-like fashion, turns on some of those who accompanied him in his rebellion, and this is how the wounded man suffered his fate. After the young man dies, Dymer wanders again, remorseful and contemplative. In his sorrow, he notices the beauty of the natural world around him; it is enough to give him some respite from the sadness he has experienced. Then he notices a lark, and a moment later he hears the crack of a gun and the lark falls dead. Dymer, saddened yet further, makes his way to a house with a belfry whose clock is not working, and the garden so overgrown blocks all sight and suggestion of the outside world. There Dymer meets a magician who drugs him, prompting him to

[24]Lewis, *Of Other Worlds*, 20.

dream salacious dreams. Dymer succumbs, only to discover the spell is being foisted upon him; the dreams are not real. Dymer resists and is shot by the magician. Wounded and wandering, he comes upon a goddess, who gives perspective to all Dymer has so far endured. He leaves to face his fate. He must engage in battle with the offspring he produced from the tryst that occurred at the castle. Dymer is killed, and following his death all nature awakens and flourishes. Here, the story ends. Now, I will recount a sampling of details from within the story that support the thesis that Lewis is imaginatively developing the theme: reality is iconoclastic.

"REALITY IS ICONOCLASTIC" DEPICTED IN *DYMER*

Continuity and change, a cousin of the iconoclastic nature of reality, is one of the threads woven throughout the fabric of *Dymer*. Change, of some sort, will constantly be required of Dymer during his adventures. New discoveries demand an adjustment of any present conceptual framework. *Whatever I once thought will be subject to modification.* These moments of disequilibrium signal the very need for change. *What kind of change is required? Do I need a change of kind, utterly rejecting my past way of thinking, or should it be a change of degree as I assimilate the new and incorporate it into a growing understanding?* The new awareness and the accompanying change, helpful as it may be, also presents another fresh and related challenge. *If I hold too tightly to the newly acquired image, it will begin to compete against a growing understanding and retard any further development.* Reality must act as the iconoclast once again.[25] Change, for mutable and thus potentially developing creatures, will always be necessary. This idea, which will echo throughout the corpus of Lewis, has its first great expression in this canto of *Dymer*.

Lewis introduces the reader to Dymer, the young inhabitant of this tyrannical city. The city was an attempt to build the utopian ideal of Plato's *Republic*. The Platonists have built this city, forcing their ideas into brick

[25]Lewis, *Surprised by Joy*, 167.

and mortar: "They laid / The strong foundations, torturing into stone / Each bubble that the Academy had blown."[26] By indicating the incongruities of "bubbles forced into stone," Lewis makes his judgment clear; there is nonsense in the endeavor. Theories of the universe are *not* the universe. These theories may represent the best thoughts one may have of a given tract of reality, but they are not to be confused for last words or final expressions of what the world *is* or *ought* to be ultimately. What finite individual or oligarchy can exercise such control and avoid all the risk of evil? Those like Dymer, who question the present order of things, are a threat to the city's existing order. Furthermore, those who ask questions or challenge convention are defined as rebels. The goal of this city is conformity and uniformity. The utopia becomes a dystopia. The inhabitants with scorn label their world "the Perfect City." Lewis's emphasis is on the artificiality, and pretense, this city has become.

Lewis describes the unnaturalness of the City and its effects on Dymer:

> For nineteen years they worked upon his soul,
> Refining, chipping, moulding and adorning.
> Then came the moment that undid the whole—
> The ripple of rude life without a warning.
> It came in lecture-time one April morning
> —Alas for laws and locks, reproach and praise,
> Who ever learned to censor the spring days?[27]

The contrast of the real spring day with the pretense of the false and forged city is explicit. This particular spring day was real; the city was spectral. Dymer sees the vision of the world cast by his teachers is a false one. He will have no more of it.

One is struck by the fact that though the "conditioners" and planners of the city seek to indoctrinate Dymer to their vision of life, and though they worked for nineteen years "refining, chipping, moulding" him to be what

---

[26]Lewis, *Dymer*, I.4.
[27]Lewis, *Dymer*, I.7.

they want him to be; it only took one moment of real life to overturn the falsehood. While being told what to think, a gentle breeze from the outside world reaches his cheek through an open window. A brown bird perches on the sill, and Dymer is stirred. The images are particularized, seemingly insignificant but real and, therefore, great contrasts to what he is hearing in the lecture hall. He laughs aloud at the absurdity—a proper response—the real he now sees makes nonsense of the lecture. The teacher seeks to silence him. Dymer, disappointed by the falsehood he has had to endure, and acting with the impetuousness of youth, strikes the lecturer dead and bolts from the city. "Down the white street and past the gate and forth / Beyond the wall he came to grassy places."[28] The street of the city is colorless and unreal, whereas the image of "grassy places" suggests greenness, nature, life, and growth.

Dymer hears music and, following it, finds that it leads him to embrace emotions otherwise long suppressed by the unrealities of the city. Again, this revealing of the subject's emotions is characteristic of secondary epic. The music is also emblematic of the real world he is now discovering, a world so different from the one he has left behind. The music feeds his imagination and caters to his sense of wonder, long stifled by the machinations of the Platonists. Lewis observes:

> That music could have crumbled proud belief
> With doubt, . . .
> And turn the young man's feet to pilgrimage—
> So sharp it was, so sure a path it found,
> Soulward with stabbing wounds of bitter sound.[29]

Dymer's soul is awakening from these deadening indoctrinations. The city stifled his soul; now, the objective world awakens him to real life. He follows a path through the woods and eventually comes to a manor house or castle. He enters, and finds it empty.

In Canto II, Lewis develops the theme further as *undeception*. While in the castle, several depictions reveal Dymer's growing surrender to reality.

---

[28]Lewis, *Dymer*, I.13.
[29]Lewis, *Dymer*, I.24.

As Dymer bolts from the falsehood and pretense of the city, in this canto he must bolt from the falsehoods and pretense that exist in his own inflated image of himself.

First, as he enters the castle, he is startled by the image of a man. Thinking a challenger is confronting him, he sets himself up for a fight, only to discover he was looking at a mirror. Recognizing himself in the mirror, he smiles before it, "wondering like a child." Here, Lewis posits "wonder" as a proper response to finding things as they are, as contrasted with a lack of wonder when one is merely projecting, and in full control of the manufactured image. This is a foretaste of what will occur later in the poem.

Second, in stanza 10, Dymer looks again into the mirror:

Till suddenly he started with surprise,
Catching, by chance, his own familiar eyes,
Fevered, yet still the same, without their share
Of bravery, undeceived and watching there.[30]

Though Dymer sees himself in this mirror, Lewis makes the point that one glance at an object is never enough. The real world in which Dymer now finds himself demands more from him. He is "undeceived" and far less courageous than he first assumed. Nevertheless, this mere moment of undeception and self-awareness is only temporary; he will have an occasion for more undeceiving to come.

Third, as Dymer leaves the mirror to continue his exploration of the castle, Lewis says, "The boy went on . . . manly playing / At manhood,"[31] suggesting that the hero of the poem still lacks what it is he must become. As the story continues, Dymer enters a chamber in the night and discovers "the breathing body of a girl." Overcome with selfish desire, he sleeps with her. There is a premonition that consequences will follow from this act, for Lewis writes it has "sent the young wolves thirsting after blood."[32]

---

[30]Lewis, *Dymer*, II.10.
[31]Lewis, *Dymer*, II.12.
[32]Lewis, *Dymer*, II.32-33.

Fourth, in his experience in the castle and in what immediately follows Dymer quickly discovers that the real world is one fraught with pain. He awakens from his night of rapture, wondering where he is and what it was that happened the night before. He leaves the castle impulsively, and Lewis adds, "Out of the unscythed grass the nettle grew."[33] The green grass of spring that once symbolized his escape from the city has now sprouted nettles. Here, suddenly he realizes the self-centeredness of his act the night before. He failed even to learn the name of the maiden. His carnal rapture was not about a relationship between two people with all of its objective complexity, but was the mere satisfying of appetite without respect for this other person, whoever she was. In denying her the dignity she deserved, that is, in denying her humanity, his own humanity has been diminished. Consequently, he begins to feel guilty. This is something that did not occur to him when he murdered his teacher. The guilt is a sign he is encountering a more complex grasp of reality. His conscience is awakening.

He returns to the manor in hope of finding the young woman. To his dismay, he only finds an immense old hag waiting at the door. He tries desperately to enter the castle again in order to find the young woman, who is fast becoming his idealized beloved. Unfortunately, every entrance is blocked and barred by the hag. He is initially filled with bravado, vowing to rescue the maiden; but his courage fails him. He is further undeceived. He begs the hag to let him enter, and she strikes Dymer, wounding him on his heart. Defeated, Dymer staggers away from the castle and wanders into the wood thinking about his beloved. Lewis's former student and biographer, George Sayer, observes, "Much of the rest of the poem is the story of his quest for her, for a being of whose nature he knows very little."[34] Certainly, this is partially true, but not utterly. Dymer is also questing for

---

[33]Lewis, *Dymer*, III, 8.
[34]George Sayer, "C. S. Lewis's *Dymer*," *Seven: An Anglo-American Literary Review* 1 (March 1980), 103.

his true self. That is, he must discover his place in the objective world around him. He must discover the true nature of the world that exists in-dependent of his thoughts and perceptions about it. The continuity of his development as a character depends upon an accurate grasp of his world. He must break free of the self-referential and utilitarian and become self-aware and empathetic.

Lewis develops the iconoclast theme further in Canto IV. Dymer makes another horrifying discovery. The reality is that his escape from the City had consequences he never intended. The reality and pain of the real world become more profound and pronounced, leading to Dymer's increased self-awareness. Having turned away from the castle, Dymer comes upon a man wounded, moaning, and blinded, lying near death. Dymer seeks to comfort him, and asks to hear his story. The man says that he once lived in "the Perfect City" where all had been well until the day that a rebel named Dymer "at one blow / Brought ruin on us all."[35] Dymer is shocked as the wounded man projects onto him motives that were not his. Lewis has Dymer see in this dying man's story the consequences of his own im-petuous act. The man continues to project his contempt onto Dymer, un-aware that it is Dymer who is now acting as his father confessor. Here, Dymer is forced to see himself as others have seen him. There is realization that one's sense of self cannot be fully realized in isolation from others. Lewis's lifelong friend and fellow Inkling, Owen Barfield, wrote, "The ex-perience of oneself over against that which is not oneself is a *sine qua non* of human consciousness."[36] Remorse for what has occurred in the wake of his bolt from the city moves him. Dymer listens quietly to the man's tale. There are incongruities between the man's story depicting Dymer as a mere rebel and the reality as Dymer perceived it. Nevertheless, Dymer is silent; he does not seek to defend himself. This sets the stage for the introduction of Bran, an actual rebel, who calls others to join him in the destruction of

---

[35]Lewis, *Dymer*, IV.16.
[36]Owen Barfield, *Owen Barfield on C. S. Lewis*, ed. G. B. Tennyson and Jane Hipolito (Oxford: Barfield Press, 2011), 46.

the City, shouting Dymer's name as a rallying cry.[37] Bran is not guided by objective, transcendent values, nor does he respect any real community to bring checks and balances into his life. He was not motivated by an awareness of spring days, or birds roosting on windowsills. He does not have anyone's welfare in mind but his own, nor does he look beyond himself for some source of moral guidance. He is truly an anarchist: "And at his heels a hundred murderers ran, / With prisoners now, clamouring to take and try them / And burn them, wedge their nails up, crucify them."[38] Lewis shows the mindlessness of the rebellion and the self-referential rhetoric of its leader, who "with maddening words dethrones the mind of men." The motivation of these rebels is nothing more than "doom and strong delusion."[39] Dymer is told, "Wherever the most shame / Was done the doer called on Dymer's name."[40] The dying man explains that Bran's tyrannies were such that he would even turn on his own, and that he himself was a victim of Bran's violence. The man wishes he had health and could avenge himself on Dymer for the harm he has suffered. Dymer stays by his side until he dies. Lewis contrasts Dymer's flight with Bran's destruction of the city. Dymer seeks escape into the real, while Bran tries to assert his will and destroy. Bran's approach is portrayed as evil. He is a precursor to the more developed villains in Lewis's mature work. He is self-referential and utilitarian; he will use anyone and any means to force his own will on the world around him. As for Dymer, he was *undeceived* in the recognition of his cowardice in Canto III, and in the discovery of the consequences of his bolt from the city.

A NEW CHALLENGE

Skipping ahead to Cantos VI and VII, Lewis develops his theme further. Dymer sets out in hope of a new beginning. He says, "Pack up the dreams

---

[37]Lewis, *Dymer,* IV.23-30.
[38]Lewis, *Dymer,* IV.28.
[39]Lewis, *Dymer,* IV.29.
[40]Lewis, *Dymer,* IV.30.

and let the life begin."[41] Once again, he notices it is spring; this part of his pilgrimage is linked with his original act of stepping out of the city on a spring day. Then, with a jarring shock, Dymer hears the firing of a gun. He rushes off to investigate and comes to another house. It is hidden behind a "yew hedge," a house with a clock tower, but "a clock that had no hands and told no hour."[42] The clock signals that Dymer is stepping into a place where the time of the real world is of no consequence. It foreshadows what he will find at the house, for its master—a magician who traffics in dreams— dwells in a world out of time. As he arrives at the house, the magician asks if Dymer heard his gun, announcing without remorse that he killed the lark. Dymer is horrified at this news, and speaks of his sorrow. The magician justifies his heinous act, saying that the singing of these birds interrupts his dreams.[43] George Sayer underscores what the reader has already discerned: "everything about the Master [of the house] is evil."[44] The magician has chosen the world of pseudoreality in pursuit of his dreams. Clearly, Lewis is drawing the sharp contrast between Dymer's escape into the real world and the magician's escape from it.

The magician feeds his newly arrived guest and then Dymer, falling under a spell, drowsily tells of his experiences up to that point. The magician has no interest in the story of the city, or Bran's rebellion, or the young, dying man; he only wants to hear of the woman Dymer encountered in the castle. As Professor Chad Walsh notes, "The magician has no interest in the visible world except as an entrance into the invisible."[45] The magician tells Dymer that he can teach him the art of dreaming so that he will be able to have the woman whenever he wants her. At this moment, the two argue. Dymer, not yet fallen fully under the magician's spell, says, "Dreams? I have had my dream too long. I thought / The sun rose for my sake."[46] The

[41]Lewis, *Dymer*, VI.2.
[42]Lewis, *Dymer*, VI.5.
[43]Lewis, *Dymer*, VI.10.
[44]Sayer, "C. S. Lewis's *Dymer*," 108.
[45]Chad Walsh, *The Literary Legacy of C. S. Lewis* (New York: Harcourt Brace Jovanovich, 1979), 47.
[46]Lewis, *Dymer*, VI.23.

difference between Dymer's quest for the real and the magician's for the self-referential are sharply contrasted. The magician, valuing control over others, seeks to further his own interests. Consequently, the magician seeks to persuade Dymer that his true fulfillments lie not in a realm inhabited by an actual woman but rather in the dream world. There he, too, can have control over his circumstances, insuring that he will meet the woman whenever he chooses. This idea is confusing to Dymer, but he is weak. The magician has baited his trap and nearly caught his prey: "The Master smiled. 'You are in haste! / For broken dreams the cure is, Dream again / And deeper.'"[47] Dymer, still sorrowing over the report of Bran and the rebellion he inspired, asks the magician if these dreams can wipe out "blood-guilt-iness" and "undo what's done amiss, / And bid the thing that has been be no more?"[48] Dymer is willing to do whatever will help him ease his sorrows. His pain is real and the dreams are not; nevertheless, to salve his guilt artificially, Dymer is persuaded to enter into the magician's world of falsehoods. Moreover, the magician takes full advantage of this opportunity, and says that the things Dymer longs for can only be found in dreams:

> "In dreams the fool is free from scorning voices.
> Grey-headed whores are virgin there again. . . .
> There the stain
> Of oldest sins—how do the good words go?—
> Though they were scarlet, shall be white as snow."[49]

Dymer desires to fix that which is broken in him. The magician by contrast has no awareness of his moral deficiencies. He is in denial of all that is real. Dymer, longing to restore his broken soul, cannot find what he is looking for in a world of make-believe. A reader cannot help but wonder what was on Lewis's mind as he wrote this. He seems to portray, accurately, the desire of anyone such as Dymer who would like to set right the things he has done,

[47]Lewis, *Dymer,* VI.24.
[48]Lewis, *Dymer,* VI.24-25.
[49]Lewis, *Dymer,* VI.26.

especially if his acts resulted in hurt to others. Dymer longs to have his sins atoned for. The magician says only dreams can set things right. Again, what was Lewis thinking about such matters, at this time in his own life? Did he have such regrets? Did he think the regrettable could be atoned for? Alternatively, was it the destiny of fallen men to live alone and isolated in the consequences of past sins? There is really, at this point, no way to know. What is clear is that he is imaginatively depicting this struggle in Dymer's story, and it is Dymer's struggle depicted, not Lewis's. Moreover, for Dymer it is a struggle of conscience awakened by tensions in the real world. At this point in the poem the magician says that guilt is merely a dream; it has no point of reference in an artificial world of dreams and imaginings.

Dymer, nearly persuaded by the magician's manipulations, comes again to his senses by thoughts of his beloved. He would much rather remain in the waking world if he knew that he might see her again. He would muster whatever "courage" was necessary if he could be assured of his goal. At the mere mention of courage, the magician begins discounting the benefits of virtue. He scoffs at the character necessary to live in the objective world. In fact, he tries to prevent Dymer from developing any kind of virtue whatsoever. In time, Dymer succumbs to the persistence of the magician who has prepared a sleeping potion for him. Just before he gives in to the power of the dreaming spell, he says to the magician, "Oh, lies, all lies . . . Why did you kill the lark?"[50] Dymer remembers the real world as he slips into unconsciousness.

As Dymer falls under the magician's spell, Lewis makes the magician's evil intent explicit: "He laughed out loud / Only once: then looked round him, hushed and cowed."[51] Like a man having something to hide, he gloats at the spell under which he has put his victim, but only as he first looks around to see that no watching eye observes his deed. His reaction indicates two things: first, he has clearly violated any kind of transcendent value and seems to know it. Second, he looks over his shoulder in fear of being found out, indicating that he knows his act against Dymer is evil. While Dymer

---

[50]Lewis, *Dymer,* VI.36.
[51]Lewis, *Dymer,* VII.3.

sleeps, the magician, "like the dog returning to his vomit," goes to his book-shelves.[52] These shelves are full of the books and tools of his necromancy. Lewis makes clear that the magician is a "lost soul" not willing to be content within his own misery; he must make others miserable as well.[53]

With all of this working against him, Dymer stirs from his dream, and waking, he cries out one word, "Water!"[54] It is thirst for water, from the real world, that breaks the dream-spell. This actual longing brings Dymer back to his senses. He drinks one glass and asks immediately for another, em-phasizing how simply his illusions can be corrected. Reality is iconoclastic. As he drinks, Dymer chides the magician, saying his world of dreams is "all lies!" The magic is "all accursed."[55] He tells the magician that it was wrong to send him to the world of dreams, for "I sought a living spirit and found instead / Bogies and wraiths."[56] The explicit image makes the contrast very clear: Dymer has grown, through all his misadventures, to prefer the real to the artificial.

The magician, practiced at ignoring reality and unmoved by Dymer's chiding, simply asks to hear about the dream. What motivates the ma-gician to make such a request? He may be seeking to woo Dymer back into the world from which he has just escaped. Perhaps his senses, so dulled by evil, are now addicted to falsehood; any report from the dream world is more highly valued than things in the real. Again, like a dog returning to its vomit, the magician grovels for whatever grubs will satisfy his palate. Oddly enough, in a manner incongruous with his contempt for the ma-gician, Dymer complies and begins to tell the story of his dream. Of course, his story is necessary for the continuance of the narrative, but it is an awkward moment in the poem. Lewis gives no reason why Dymer should grant the magician's request. Nevertheless, Dymer shares his dream. Undeceived, he knows these dreams were nothing more than his own

[52]Lewis, *Dymer,* VII.7.
[53]Lewis, *Dymer,* VII.9.
[54]Lewis, *Dymer,* VII.11.
[55]Lewis, *Dymer,* VII.11.
[56]Lewis, *Dymer,* VII.12.

imaginative projections. He says, "I was making everything I saw, / Too
sweet, far too well fitted to desire / To be a living thing."[57] At this point,
Dymer desperately wants the world as it is, with all of its risks and dangers.
He prefers the real to all that is false and made up. The Dymer who left the
artificialities of "the Perfect City" would now equally escape those artificialities of his own imagination. Dymer is maturing. All of this has some
degree of continuity with where he has been before.

Again, whether he is addicted to the dream world or merely desires to
ensnare Dymer in another trap, the magician asks if Dymer found the
woman he sought in the dream. After affirming that she was there, the
magician asks, "Was she not fair?" then adds, "Almost a living soul."[58]
Again, he seeks to persuade Dymer to prefer the unreal to the real. Dymer
sees through the magician's manipulative rhetoric and refuses to take the
bait. He objects to the magician's world of dreams, noting,

> But every part
> Was what I made it—all that I had dreamed—
> No more, no less: the mirror of my heart,
> Such things as boyhood feigns beneath the smart
> Of solitude and spring. I was deceived.[59]

Dymer continues to recount his dream for the magician. He speaks of the
lady's words to him: "Her sweetness drew / A veil before my eyes."[60] She seeks
to woo by saying that "the shadow-lands of earth" were really only loved in
desire for the world of the dream. She falsely claims that the real world is
only a substitute. She tells Dymer that he has at last come to his home, and
she begins to worship him. It is at this point that Dymer asks the moral
question and brings matters of good and evil into the arena: "Is it not wrong
/ That men's delusions should be made so strong?"[61] The temptation to

[57]Lewis, *Dymer*, VII.18.
[58]Lewis, *Dymer*, VII.20.
[59]Lewis, *Dymer*, VII.20.
[60]Lewis, *Dymer*, VII.21.
[61]Lewis, *Dymer*, VII.23.

succumb to the dream is strong in him, but a moment comes when the spell
is at last broken. Though he has been "nearly wrecked," Dymer says,

> She went too fast. Soft to my arms she came.
> The robe slipped from her shoulder. The smooth breast
> Was bare against my own. She shone like flame
> Before me in the dusk, all love, all shame—
> Faugh!—and it was myself.[62]

In realizing the truth that the woman in his dream is nothing but his own
projection, Dymer breaks free of the spell finally, and asks for water. Here,
Lewis begins to tie the various parts of the poem together. The woman in the
dream is of his own manufacture. The dream is not unlike "the Perfect City,"
which was the manufacture of the Platonists' dreams and bubbles tortured
into stone. Both were equally false notions of reality. It was necessary for
Dymer to escape the unreality of the City, and now this world of dreams.
Something as simple as spring awakened him from the one world, and now
something as simple as a thirst for water awakens him from the other.

As Dymer sets out to leave the house, the magician raises his gun and
shoots him. The events at the magician's house begin with the shooting of
the lark—the destruction of any reality that threatens the magician's dream
world—and in the end the magician shoots Dymer because his developing
commitments to the real world are also a threat to the magician. He will have
his way. His uncorrected falsehoods sustain him in his evil acts. He does not
value others, only himself. He lacks piety and a sense of justice. He is inca-
pable of rendering to others their due, he prefers to destroy the living in order
to maintain the artificial. His place in Dymer's story is to deepen Dymer's
grasp of the consequences of suppressing the inexorable demands of reality.

ANOTHER DISCOVERY STILL TO MAKE

Wounded, Dymer is ever more sensitive to the objective world. While it is
not visible, the wind is more real than the things he has encountered in the

---

[62]Lewis, *Dymer*, VII.25.

two preceding cantos. In his escape into the real, Dymer sees another clock
and notices the detail that it strikes the quarter of the hour. He has escaped
the dreams of the magician's house, whose faceless clock has no hands and
whose world is out of beat with the objective world, to discover a clock
whose time is measured and precise. As he travels on with "thundering
pain," the fog from the magician's house clears and he sees the clouds break
and the night sky "Spacious with sudden stars."[63] These are real stars in a
wide, wide sky, unlike the stifling make-believe world of the dreams.
Though wounded, he has escaped.

In this real world, he is surprised to come upon the actual woman he
has been seeking all along. He asks if she is "The loved one, the long lost,"
and staring at her, asks "Truly?" She replies, "Truly indeed."[64] This again
establishes the reality of the world where Dymer finds himself, and it contrasts with the world of the magician from which he has just come. Still he
has his doubts. He wants to be sure that the woman is not "one more
phantom to beguile." The reality of this experience is marked by the fact
that the clock's bell "Tolled out another quarter."[65] Dymer asks that she
leave him, for he suspects that she is a god who cannot understand all he
has suffered. Not denying she is a deity, she corrects him and says, "The
gods themselves know pain, the eternal forms."[66] She says she is, in fact,
familiar with pain and suffering. He wants to know if it was the gods who
called him out of the city and if so, has he sinned by following them. He
does not give her time to answer before he asks, what for him, is the more
important question: "Must things of dust / Guess their own way in the
dark?" To which she answers, "They must."[67] Dymer responds in wrath,
wanting to know why she has come "in human shape, in sweet disguise /
Wooing me, lurking for me in my path / . . . Snared me with shows of
love—and all was lies." The answer is difficult for Dymer, for the goddess

[63]Lewis, *Dymer,* VIII.3-4.
[64]Lewis, *Dymer,* VIII.6.
[65]Lewis, *Dymer,* VIII.7.
[66]Lewis, *Dymer,* VIII.9.
[67]Lewis, *Dymer,* VIII.12.

says, "Our kind must come to all / If bidden, but in the shape for which they call."[68] She eventually tells him that he must now "Go forth; the journey is not ended yet." The goddess reveals to Dymer the very purpose for his journey. She says that certainly he has already imagined himself dead and "on the bier" many times before; that in fact, Dymer has slain himself every hour. It is an enigma, but as Dymer turns to question the goddess further, she is gone.[69]

In a passage prefiguring much of Lewis's mature work, Dymer reflects on the fact that there have been many Dymers. Yet life's experiences, every new encounter with reality, have lain to rest each Dymer for another one who was yet emerging. He speculates about his own pilgrimage:

"There was a Dymer once who worked and played
About the City; I sloughed him off and ran.
There was a Dymer in the forest glade
Ranting alone, skulking the fates of man.
I cast him also, and a third began
And he too died. But I am none of those.
Is there another still to die . . . Who knows?"[70]

Dymer is growing. He experiences continuity and change. His life is becoming more real and authentic. He is in process. What is emerging is continually being defined and redefined by his adjustment to reality. A final word has not been uttered about him, just as it cannot be uttered about any man. Helen Joy Davidman visited Lewis for the Christmas holidays in 1952. Lewis wrote in her copy of *The Great Divorce*, "There are three images in my mind which I must continually forsake and replace by better ones: the false image of God, the false image of my neighbours, and the false image of myself. C. S. Lewis 30 December 1952 (from an unwritten chapter on Iconoclasm)."[71] Even though this chapter was

---

[68]Lewis, *Dymer*, VIII.13.
[69]Lewis, *Dymer*, VIII.19-20.
[70]Lewis, *Dymer*, VIII.24.
[71]Walter Hooper, *C. S. Lewis: A Companion Guide* (San Francisco: Harper Collins, 1996), 61.

yet unwritten, it would appear that it was, in some ways, anticipated by this canto in *Dymer*.

Dymer struggles to get to a "belfried place." He passes through an old gate and finds himself in a cemetery. The portent of another death, and the wonder of what new Dymer may yet emerge, is here anticipated. Dymer meets a sentry in that place who is guarding against the intrusion of a monster. The sentry tells Dymer the tale of the beast's origin, and, to his shock, Dymer discovers that he is the father. The monster is the offspring of the tryst with the woman in the castle. For some reason, which Lewis never fully provides, Dymer decides that he must either slay the beast or be slain by it.[72] As the dawn breaks and the beast arrives, Dymer sees that the region is "a ruinous land."[73] He faces the beast and it kills him in an instant. In that very moment "came the rising sun," and with it the "ruinous land" sprouts forth vegetation, and the brute becomes a god.[74] Thus ends the story of Dymer. In his preface to the 1950 edition of the poem, Lewis says of Dymer, "Hunger and a shock of real danger bring him to his senses and he at last accepts reality."[75]

A CONCLUDING WORD ABOUT *DYMER*

Even though the consequences of his past sins haunt him, Dymer grows by virtue of his honesty. With all of his mistakes and failures, he nevertheless looks at the real world and accommodates himself to it. He chooses to redress his wrongs and accepts his fate by facing the monster whose very existence is the consequence of indulgent fantasies. The non-Christian Lewis has Dymer atone for his own sins. Nothing approximates vicarious atonement in this book. Nevertheless, Dymer's choice to face reality, even if such a choice reveals flaws of character, is presented as a likely aid to set him on a right track. In his introduction to *The Great Divorce*, Lewis notes

---

[72]Lewis, *Dymer*, IX.15.
[73]Lewis, *Dymer*, IX.24.
[74]Lewis, *Dymer*, IX.30-34.
[75]Preface, 14.

when one sets out on a wrong road there is no making it the right road, any more than wrong figures can lead to a right sum. The only way to begin the process of fixing the error is to acknowledge the mistake and go back where it can be set right. "Evil can be undone, but it cannot 'develop' into good."[76] In *Dymer*, Lewis first depicts this imaginatively.

The objective demands of reality, the awareness of moral responsibility, and the consequences for one's actions are all features in evidence in the poem. These ideas seem to be looming in the background whenever Lewis is telling a story. It is true of the pre-Christian Lewis as well as the postconverted Lewis. For the student of Lewis, *Dymer* is the beginning and has continuity with what will follow.

Lewis would come to believe the Christian story was anticipated in the early pre-Christian myths.[77] There is no reason not to suppose that Lewis's myth may also suggest what is coming. Lewis depicts Dymer as being undeceived by reality repeatedly. In some ways, even the pre-Christian Lewis may unwittingly have provided a template for the reader to think about undeception in his or her own life. Any true encounter with reality can open doors to discover whatever might be behind it. Lewis had not come to such a place in his own life when he wrote *Dymer*. Nevertheless, he did prepare an edition for republication in 1950, nearly a quarter of a century after the original publication. Why did he do this? Perhaps the Christian Lewis saw something beyond the modest literary merits of the poem that transcended any value he could have imagined when he wrote it. If this may be so, it is most likely found in the big idea that "reality is iconoclastic."

In *The Great Divorce*, George MacDonald's character says that heaven and hell are retrospective, for each works backward to transform what has gone on before. Something of heaven or hell will be evident in all of life's experience in the end, "The good man's past begins to change so that his forgiven sins and remembered sorrows take on the quality of Heaven: the bad man's past already conforms to his badness and is filled

[76]C. S. Lewis, *The Great Divorce* (New York: Macmillan, 1950), vi.
[77]C. S. Lewis, *Mere Christianity* (London: Geoffrey Bles, 1953), 29.

with dreariness."[78] Could something like this also be apparent in *Dymer*? Furthermore, in *Mere Christianity*, Lewis notes, "If you are a Christian you do not have to believe that all the other religions are simply wrong all through."[79] Equally, it should not be supposed everything in the pre-Christian Lewis must be overshadowed or discounted by the writings of the converted Lewis. There is in this story "a splendour in the dark, a tale, a song," and there are many notes at play in Lewis's early work anticipating the themes of his later material. This will be the subject of the next two chapters. First, it was necessary, here, to know something of the story of *Dymer* as it is.

---

[78]Lewis, *The Great Divorce*, 64.
[79]Lewis, *Mere Christianity*, 29.

RESPONSE

Jeffry C. Davis

THE TASK BEFORE ME is to provide a thoughtful "reader's response" to the narrative poem *Dymer*, by Oxford Professor C. S. Lewis, while at the same time responding to the analysis of that work by Professor Jerry Root, briefly assessing the relative merits of both. In the company of scholars such as Don King, Malcolm Guite, and Crystal Hurd, Root recognizes *Dymer* as an "important" work of literature. To this claim I heartily respond, "Yes, I agree." From a scholarly perspective, *Dymer* represents an overlooked literary artifact by one of the most influential English writers of the twentieth century, who was certainly the greatest Christian prose writer of his age. Therefore Lewis's early poem does possess seminal significance, as Professor Root argues; and it deserves more investigation as a form of literary craft that expresses several nascent traits and themes of the man who would later become *lionized*, in the literal and the figurative sense. Professor Root, too, has become known for his own *Aslanic* tendencies, including his abiding interest in the work, and his affection for the legendary life, of that inimitable, pipe-smoking, pint-sipping, Protestant saint of the Wade Center. (Parenthetically speaking, Wheaton's love of Lewis remains as a great irony, considering that when I was an undergraduate there, and throughout my first years as a young professor of English, the campus, and indeed the whole town of Wheaton, was known for being "dry"—a trait that cannot solely be attributed to the laconic wit of Leland Ryken, longtime English professor and Lewis scholar.)

Were it not for the fact that Dr. Root possesses the virtues of being charitable and generous as a teacher, a colleague, and a friend (one of my dearest friends in the world), I would not presume to tell him, and this audience, *this* reader's response to *Dymer*—that the poem he so sincerely reveres is *not* in my estimation a great work of literature. (Professor Root, here I must remind you of a verse from the Old Testament: Proverbs 27:6—"Faithful are the wounds of a friend.") Besides being less than great literature, *Dymer* does not strike me as a text that would warmly enliven the characteristic curiosities of the typical reader of Saint Lewis (and here I am not speaking geographically).

Great literary works are recognized, in part, for their *remarkable* influence on readers. When I say "remarkable," I intend the adjective in its fullest sense, with three particular renderings.

First, remarkable means "worthy of being recognized as extraordinary." In other words, the impact of a great literary work can be perceived in a variety of uncommon or exceptional ways, possibly described by readers with the following words: "arresting," "brilliant," "commanding," "dramatic," "emphatic," "fulfilling," "groundbreaking," "harrowing," "insightful," or "jubilant." The list of distinctive qualifiers goes on, according to each reader's engagement with the text; however, a consensus generally emerges that a given work possesses attributes that are exemplary, meriting widespread and lasting recognition.

Second, to say that a literary work is "remarkable" also means that it provokes a distinctly human activity of "making meaningful remarks about it." As I regularly explain to my advanced students of English, particularly in the senior seminar, "How we respond to a work of literature is something that we should be especially mindful of, paying attention to the ways in which we, as readers, interact with each text, and how we process our experiences, both individually and socially." Such processing of our responses is vital to a full appreciation of the literary arts, and to the cultivation of humanity by those to engage them. It includes, then, taking account of the following human traits: our *cognitive* (or rational) thoughts, our *emotive* (or sentient) perceptions, and what I will call our *transflective* (or light transmitting and reflecting) considerations (borrowing a term from computing sciences, in reference to liquid crystal displays, and applying it inventively here, in an interdisciplinary manner). By the portmanteau "transflective," I mean how texts convey aspects of the transcendent.

Third, great works of literature that are remarkable *do* something to us as readers: they mark us, shaping who we are in enduring ways. And as we engage, and reengage, great texts (the hallmark of a classic—people reread them), they "re-mark" us, inscribing our sensibilities with artistic power. When great works of literature re-mark us in this way, they live on in our memory, and they affect us consciously and unconsciously, informing how we choose to live our lives.

Keeping all this in mind, I assert that *Dymer* is unqualified in its unremarkable qualities as a poem. Standing on its own merits, it has serious problems: its literary reception supports this, its poetic deficiencies confirm this, and its originator—the erstwhile poet, Lewis himself—openly acknowledges this. Nevertheless, *Dymer* is indeed important and iconoclastic, as Professor Root has suggested. (By the way, his presentation of *Dymer*—including the rendering of the basic narrative—was far better than Lewis's.) So then, *Dymer* proves to be a poem that is certainly worthy of scholarly examination, consistent with Dr. Root's argument. Most poignantly, the poem fulfilled an ironic purpose: it shattered, for Lewis, the egocentric image he had of himself as a young, proud, and unregenerate poet, whose dream was to one day become a great poet, famous among those recognized in Westminster Abbey.[1] Thus *Dymer* can be understood as a divine catalyst, in and of itself, ultimately moving Lewis away from the fantasy of self-interested poetic fame, toward the reality, and the humility, of accepting his true creative calling—primarily as a prose fiction writer.

---

[1] Ironically, on November 22, 2013, C. S. Lewis was indeed memorialized in Poet's Corner at Westminster Abbey on the fiftieth anniversary of his death. However, this recognition was a result of his extraordinary contribution to the world of literature, and not for his achievement as a poet.

The critical reviews of *Dymer,* shortly after its printing in 1926, signal a decidedly mixed literary reception. And here I interpret the historical data a bit differently than George Sayer. In the September 19, 1926, issue of *The Sunday Times,* we find the following equivocal commentary about the publication by Clive Hamilton, the pseudonym for C. S. Lewis, who was then a newly appointed Oxford don at Magdalen College, and who obviously wanted to protect his reputation as a scholar, especially from any potential bad press he might receive as an inferior poet. The *Times* critic, Dilys Powell, who at first provides a few positive words about *Dymer,* concludes by assessing Lewis's major mistake as an artist—selecting the wrong creative genre for the narrative's expression. She writes,

> The voyage of the soul in search of the spirit, its struggles with fear, with the listlessness of dreams, and its final triumph, are set forth with an unusual sureness. Of felicitous phrases there are many . . . And yet it seems to us that *Mr. Hamilton has mistaken his opportunity. The idea was not one for treatment in verse. The exigencies of the poetic line prevent such an easy sequence as the allegory demands; but as a prose tale how splendidly it would have flowed!* (emphasis added)[2]

Indeed, Professor Root's prose rendition demonstrates this truth. The critic's assessment seems uncanny in its proclamation, boldly stating that the writer should have exerted his energies not on verse, with its structured metering and formal constraints, but on prose—with its greater freedom of expression. What an apt and even prophetic appraisal!

The Spectator, a periodical known for its coverage of current British affairs and culture, circulated a modest but encouraging poetry review. The critic begins with a line that sounds strained in its praise, stating that "*Dymer, if* not so masterly, is *perhaps* better for its simplicity" (emphasis added).[3] Note that this reviewer describes the poem using a conditional dependent clause beginning with "if "; and then he follows with the adverb

---

[2] Dilys Powell, review of *Dymer, The Sunday Times* (London), September 19, 1926.
[3] C. Henry Warren, "Gems and Coloured Glass," *The Spectator* (Bloomsbury), October 30, 1926.

that is typically used to express uncertainty or doubt—"perhaps." From a grammatical standpoint, the critic creates a conditional construction, conveying some tentativeness about the poem. Yet, he does proceed with a somewhat more affirming, even reassuring, tone:

> Here is the evolution towards spiritual freedom of a young man bred in the standardized society of the Perfect City; but Mr. Hamilton objectifies his theme so effectively and dramatically that *it is not until the moving events are all done that we realize the full purport of what we have been reading*. Here is a little epic burnt out of vital experience and given to us through a poet's eye. (emphasis added)[4]

Again, pay attention to the suggestion that the reader may not truly understand the thematic significance of this "epic" even after all of the plot action has completed. This is an odd way to say, "Reader, you will need to press through with this poem to the end, at which point you may be able to gain a sense of it, once you are done." Why? The poem does not readily disclose its meaning, canto by canto. It resists intelligibility. Yet, ironically, this critic closes with something that seems inconsistent, calling *Dymer* a "lovely poem." The choice of descriptive diction could not be farther from reality. To be clear, William Shakespeare's "Sonnet 18" is a lovely poem, John Keats's "Ode to a Grecian Urn" is a lovely poem, and Elizabeth Barret Browning's "How Do I Love Thee" is a lovely poem; but C. S. Lewis's *Dymer* defies the category of a "lovely poem." Rather, this complicated verse narrative, written by the poet in his twenties while in the midst of a profound identity crisis, exhibits existential disbelief, struggle, and angst. The poem portrays a young rebel facing a difficult, opaque, and foreboding situation, with an ending that is surprising and confusing. It is not aesthetically beautiful or rhythmically pleasing. Instead, it presents a frustrating reading experience, especially for those who prefer "lovely" poems.

A critic writing for *The Poetry Review* offered an assessment of Lewis's craft that was less complimentary and more critical in his evaluation of

---

[4]Warren, "Gems and Coloured Glass."

Dymer, raising concerns about the poem's inadequacies. The reviewer states in reference to the poem, "One is *little* impressed by the allegory that is *hard to understand*, amazed at the alternate flashes of brilliance and *dullness in the style* of writing, and wholly delighted by the lyrical quality of *many [not all] of the lines*" (emphasis added).[5] Note that each of the poem's strengths is linked to a related weakness. In the end, *Dymer* proved not to be a resounding success to this critic.

One final review of the poem, published in *The Saturday Review*, a London newspaper of "politics, literature, science, and art," employs the indicative mood of grammar, expressing several negative sentiments of the critic, who pulls no punches. This critic expounds,

> As for "Dymer" the symbolism is to us not at all clear. Dymer was born in the Perfect City, a horrible utopia from which he quite naturally revolted. But his revolt led to a revolution for which he felt himself severely to blame, though he had merely run away, after, it must be said, murdering a lecturer.

Here the critic pauses to offer a bit of parenthetical commentary, with sarcasm.

> (But then there have been many lecturers we have wanted to murder!)

The critic goes on, after making jest of the plot line.

> He [Dymer] finds a remarkable palace, has an affair in the dark with a very real girl who afterwards turns out to be the spirit of Truth or some such thing, meets up with an old gentleman who dabbles in black art and turns out not to be a gentleman at all, finds out the cheat of dreams, goes to a graveyard and is translated into the super-solar, where he meets an angel sentinel who says he is guarding the way of spirits from a beast of despair. This turns out to be Dymer's progeny by the lady aforementioned. So Dymer takes [armaments] from the sentinel,

---

[5]Quoted in Philip Zaleski and Carol Zaleski, *The Fellowship: The Literary Lives of the Inklings: J. R. R. Tolkien, C. S. Lewis, Owen Barfield, and Charles Williams* (New York: Farrar, Straus and Giroux, 2015), 155.

indulges in combat with the beast, is killed by it, and the conquering brute becomes a winged and sworded shape towering to the skies![6]

The prose summation here, attempting to bring coherence to the jumbled sequence of the poetic narrative, struggles under the weight of the task. The critic concludes, "There the poem ends. . . . some good writing; but the poem as a whole does not 'jell.' . . . The mixture of realistic detail and of wandering symbolism is not successful."[7] Finally, the critic observes that the poem's phrasing is "never extraordinary."[8] In summation, the critic's concerns are these: (1) the plot of the narrative poem lacks focus, meandering here and there; (2) the overall structure is flawed, never really holding together; (3) the symbolism is unsuccessful in its presentation, without possessing semiotic lucidity; and (4) the word construction is nothing exceptional, and frankly quite ordinary throughout. These are not the *remarkable* traits of a great work of poetry, as Professor Root would have us believe. To the contrary, they accurately convey some of the inherent complications with *Dymer*, problems with which contemporary readers surely wrestle.

The tepid critical reception of Lewis's poem suggests that there are, indeed, serious problems with the craft of *Dymer*. Returning to my central assertion, the poem is rather unremarkable, apart from the associated renown of its versifier. Informed by Aristotle's theoretical perspective, as found in the *Poetics* (a work that Lewis would have been very familiar with at the time of the poem's creation), I see the major flaw of *Dymer* as being its obvious incoherence—a disjointed collection of cantos with lots of murky thoughts, dark woods, and fantastical encounters with strange beings.

First, consider the length and basic meter of the poem: nine cantos, each comprised of about thirty stanzas, for a total of 295 septets of "rhyme royal"—a metrical form used by Geoffrey Chaucer, which employs a seven-line stanza, each containing ten syllable lines, written in iambic pentameter,

[6]"The New Books—Poetry," *The Saturday Review of Literature* (London), August 13, 1927.
[7]"The New Books—Poetry."
[8]"The New Books—Poetry."

with the rhyme scheme of ABABBCC. Obviously, this medieval meter was not in vogue when Lewis chose to use it for his poem in the early twentieth century. As Lionel Adey explains, "In the 1920s, the diminishing public for long poems preferred the compressed, contextless utterance and varied meters of the *Waste Land* to narrative in rhyme royal."[9] Still, Lewis, by my count, places approximately eighteen thousand words into over two thousand lines of this archaic verse form. As Adey observes, Lewis's poetic craft could not compete with the innovation of contemporaries like Pound, Eliot, and Yeats.[10]

Keep in mind, also, that *Dymer* is characterized as an epic—a long narrative poem recounting the adventures of a hero. Aristotle avers that an epic plot should naturally emerge out of the continuous action of the central character, resulting in an organic poetic structure, one possessing wholeness. "A poetic imitation, then," explains Aristotle, "ought to be unified."[11] But *Dymer* appears more disjointed than unified. As Alister McGrath explains, "The whole is somehow not equal to its parts. Its few shards of brilliance are not sustained and are overwhelmed by the expanses of lacklustre and flat lines. *Dymer*, considered as a poem, simply does not work."[12]

In Canto I, the voice of the narrator-poet describes the function of the poem much like a social contract: "We begin / A partnership where both must toil to hold / The clue that I caught first. We lose or win / Together; if you read, you are enrolled."[13] In other words, as the initial lines suggest, to be a reader of this poem is to be enlisted in the hard work of making sense of it. However, immediately the presumed partnership between writer and reader becomes strained because of the plot's asymmetrical development. A truncated beginning portrays Dymer committing a violent murder—an

---

[9]Lionel Adey, *C. S. Lewis: Writer, Dreamer, and Mentor* (Grand Rapids, MI: Eerdmans, 1998), 201.

[10]Adey, *C. S. Lewis*, 200.

[11]Aristotle, *Poetics*, trans. Gerald F. Else (Ann Arbor: University of Michigan Press, 1970), 32.

[12]Alister McGrath, *C. S. Lewis—A Life: Eccentric Genius, Reluctant Prophet* (Carol Stream, IL: Tyndale, 2013), 107-8.

[13]Lewis, *Dymer*, I.2. Cf. C. S. Lewis, *The Collected Poems of C. S. Lewis: A Critical Edition*, ed. Don W. King (Kent, OH: Kent State University Press, 2015), 149.

Aristotelian act of *hamartia*—all within the first ten stanzas, well before the reader has had time to acclimate to the setting, much less gain a sympathetic understanding of the protagonist, which I argue never really occurs. And so the plot unfolds in the meandering muddle of the middle part of the poem: Dymer roams from the Platonic school of his slain teacher, to the forest of sexual indulgence with a girl, to a palace defended by a gnarled old woman (actually the morphing spirit-being of his lover), to a conversation with a handless and footless man about revolution, to a moment of self-recrimination for a deed done impetuously, to a magician who tempts him to indulge in dreams for reenacted pleasure, to the unexpected moment of the maniac magician's gunshot and impending mortality, to the painful reckoning with his illusory ambitions and indulgent self. The ending portrays Dymer in a great battle with the beast of his own making, in the throes of death, fighting the monster. Like the *Iliad*'s Hektor, in his battle with Achilles outside the ramparts of Troy, Dymer throws his spear and misses, after which he raises his sword and shield for mortal combat. At this point, the narrator-poet surprisingly, abruptly, interrupts the action of the poem, much to the reader's chagrin: "What now, my friends? You get no more from me / Of Dymer. He goes out from us."[14] This *deus ex machina* moment jarringly disrupts the narrative flow of the poem. Such an epic aberration is, as Aristotle indicates, a departure from mimetic craft. "The poet should do as little of the talking as possible," states Aristotle.[15] As a result of this interruption, the reader feels cheated with regard to the original terms of the contract established at the outset. The lasting overall impression of the poem's plot movement remains episodic and entangled. "With all its formal intricacies," concludes Luci Shaw regarding *Dymer*'s organizational structure, "it was unevenly conceived and executed. It is difficult to describe the theme of *Dymer*, let alone interpret it."[16]

Lewis, *Dymer*, IX.29.
15Aristotle, *Poetics*, 65.
16Quoted in Don W. King, *C. S. Lewis, Poet: The Legacy of His Poetic Impulse* (Kent, OH: Kent State University Press, 2001), 137.

Finally, Lewis himself acknowledges his own ambivalence about the merit of *Dymer* in his 1950 preface to the second publication of the poem. There he confesses, with astonishing self-effacement, much like a modern-day Augustine, "*Dymer*, like many better books, found some good reviews . . . and almost no readers. The idea of disturbing its repose in the grave, now, comes from the publishers, not from me."[17] Compare these mature reflections, representing the Christian version of Lewis, with the following pre-Christian reflections, which come from an entry in his personal diary, right around the time that *Dymer* was rejected by the publisher Heinemann. The young aspiring poet writes to himself,

> I desire that my value as a poet should be acknowledged by others.
> . . . I have flattered myself with the idea of being among my own people when I was reading [the great English poets], and it is un-pleasing to have to stand down and take my place in the crowd. . . .
> The only healthy, or happy, or eternal life is to look so steadily on the World that the representation "Me" fades away.[18]

What a profound realization from a man hungry to be accepted by the literati of his day. Yet, his internal wrestling with his own demons of desire, channeled through his early attempt at self-made immortality through poetic success, gradually fades away. Shortly before his conversion, Lewis writes to his friend Arthur Greeves, consoling him after he had just gone through the disappointing experience of having a piece of his writing rejected. He explains to Greeves that throughout his entire early adult life, he had one single ambition—to become a poet, a great poet. This pursuit, he admits, took control of his thoughts and actions—taking over as a form of idolatry, until God began to supplant it.

Lewis explains how this idolatrous behavior diminished—through rejection and grief. The inability to get what he wanted, what he thought he

---

[17]Preface, 9.
[18]C. S. Lewis, *The Letters of C. S. Lewis to Arthur Greeves (1914–1963)*, ed. Walter Hooper (New York: Colliers, 1986), 383.

needed, served as a strange sort of grace, tempering his heart and sharpening his mind for things directed by the living God, later in life. Writing to Greeves, Lewis—in his early thirties—describes this unusual gift: "Suffering of the sort that you are now feeling is my special subject, my profession, my long suit, the thing I claim to be an expert in."[19] Lewis consoled Greeves with genuine spiritual encouragement, drawn from his own loss and struggle, affirming the possibility that his Creator, Greeves's Creator, might somehow be at work in such times of sorrow, treating them benevolently by preventing them from gaining renown in the realm of great poets. As Don King perceptively writes, "Such a denial saved them from the disappointment and despair attendant upon those who briefly flame up with literary fame, only to flicker quickly before fading into oblivion."[20]

As Professor Root has argued, *Dymer* demonstrates an early manifestation of the iconoclastic theme that captivated Lewis's imagination, as found throughout the works of his mature Christian life. One can only wonder what would have resulted if *Dymer* had actually succeeded, if it had won the applause of critics. What *if* it had exhibited a coherent structure, and *if* it had become a great literary work, remarkable in its artistic craft? What we know, by most accounts, is that Lewis actually failed as a poet, even by his own candid assessment. His dream was dashed, and he experienced iconoclastic disillusionment. To this ironic conclusion, all lovers of Lewis should resoundingly say, "Thank God for *Dymer!*"

---

[19] Lewis, *Letters of C. S. Lewis to Arthur Greeves*, 379.
[20] Don W. King, "C. S. Lewis, Poet," in *Bloom's Modern Critical Views: C. S. Lewis*, ed. Harold Bloom (New York: Chelsea House, 2006), 191-223; 204.

2

"THE LOW VOICE OF THE WORLD / BROODING ALONE BENEATH THE STRENGTH OF THINGS"

IN MY FIRST CHAPTER, I sought to acquaint readers with the story of C. S. Lewis's narrative poem *Dymer*. It was the only narrative poem published during his lifetime and one of only two books published before his conversion to Christianity. Lewis had hopes of becoming a poet. Unfortunately, *Dymer* was not well received and fell short of his literary expectations. This convinced Lewis he would have to make his living some other way. Nevertheless, *Dymer* does reveal something of the rigor Lewis put into cultivating his skills as a writer. He learned the economy of words and the value of carefully selecting a literary form to match what he wanted to say. These skills served him well and contributed to his success as a prose writer. While Lewis never achieved commercial success as a poet, still *Dymer* remains important as a literary artifact for all who want to understand him fully. Before it is anything else, *Dymer* is a story, and reveals something of Lewis's creative imagination. In my last chapter, I sought to set forth the story for those unacquainted with the narrative. Furthermore, I pointed out that the book has continuity with Lewis's later work. It is, in fact, an early example of one of Lewis's biggest ideas that "reality is iconoclastic."

In this chapter, I want to look at influences on Lewis as he wrote. This is not to suggest that *Dymer* is autobiography. Lewis says explicitly in a letter to his friend Arthur Greeves, "Of course I'm not Dymer."[1] Nevertheless, in his 1950 preface to the second edition of *Dymer*, he does write about various ideas that, to one degree or another, are in evidence in his poem. These influences and their effect on the manuscript are the subject of this chapter. Furthermore, *Dymer* has much in seed destined to blossom into full flower—this is in anticipation of his later work. That will be the topic of my third chapter.

LEWIS'S PREFACE TO *DYMER*

In 1950, the publisher released a second printing of *Dymer*, for which Lewis wrote a preface. With characteristic humility, he says that since the publishers sought to disturb "its repose in the grave," he felt he should "be present at the exhumation."[2] In this preface he highlights those things that changed both in him and around him, and he concedes that these things *within* and *without* had an influence on him as he wrote. There are also influences detected by internal evidence, and these are implicit in the poem itself. This includes Lewis's World War I experience. In addition, letters he wrote while working on *Dymer* reveal other influences. Furthermore, reflections preserved in his autobiography, *Surprised by Joy*, show that Lewis was also deeply affected by myth. In the preface Lewis makes explicit mention of many things that he felt would be useful to a reader of the poem. These topics are those of *escape*, the "*Christina Dreams*,"[3] the *new psychology*, and the lifelong experiences of *longing* that haunted him from childhood. I will look at each of these concepts in some detail.

---

[1] C. S. Lewis, *Dymer: Wade Annotated Edition* in Jerry Root, *Splendour in the Dark: C. S. Lewis's Dymer in His Life and Work* (Downers Grove, IL: IVP Academic 2020), 9.

[2] Preface, 9.

[3] In his Preface to the 1950 edition of *Dymer*, Lewis notes that the "Christina Dream" is taken from the character of Christina Pontifex from Samuel Butler's *The Way of All Flesh*. The spelling of "Christina" was changed to "Christiana" in *Narrative Poems*, published in 1972 after Lewis's death. See Preface, 11.

One more thing, when Lewis wrote, "This story arrived, complete, in my mind somewhere about my seventeenth year."[4] This is evidence of Lewis's pictorial imagination. He often writes about stories that seemed to appear almost full-bodied in his imagination. I am not sure even Lewis understood how this works, for he wrote, "*It came*. I doubt if we shall ever know more of the process called 'inspiration' than those two monosyllables tell us."[5] These moments of inspiration were coupled with the pleasure he took in exercising his imagination, honing his skill as a storyteller to thus produce this literary artifact.

IMPLICIT INFLUENCES ON *DYMER*

The implicit influence of World War I. There are several verses in the various cantos of *Dymer* where Lewis's war experiences seem to influence the narrative. He fought in the Battle of the Somme at Monchy-le-Preux, Fampoux, and Mont-Bernanchon. He saw, firsthand, the horrors of trench warfare. Lewis was injured and scarred for the rest of his life. Descriptions in various cantos seem to draw from his war experience. For example, Dymer's adventures bring him to a man wounded, blind, and dying. He speaks to Dymer, "Listen: I've bled too deep / To last out till the morning. I'll be dead / Within the hour—sleep then. I've heard it said / They don't mind at the last, but this is Hell. / If I'd the strength—I have such things to tell."[6]

Dymer learns this man also bolted from the City. Now blind, his arms cut off, and bleeding to death, the wounded man tells his story. Dymer is shocked to learn that in the wake of his flight from the City a rebellion broke out led by an anarchist named Bran. Bran, ascending to unchecked power, then turned on his comrades, mortally wounding this man. Unaware with whom he is speaking, the dying man curses the memory of Dymer for acts that prompted the rebellion. As Lewis describes the man's

---

[4]Preface, 9.
[5]C. S. Lewis, *Selected Literary Essays*, ed. Walter Hooper (Cambridge: Cambridge University Press, 1969), 147.
[6]Lewis, *Dymer*, IV.12-13.

condition, it is difficult not to believe that something of death in the trenches and the horrors of battle were proximate to his mind as he wrote.

Furthermore, it is likely something of his war experiences were vivid in his memory as the voice of the wounded man confesses, "Here first I heard the bullets sting the air."[7] And again,

> Like swarming bees
> Their spraying bullets came—no time for breath.
> I saw men's stomachs fall out on their knees;
> And shouting faces, while they shouted, freeze
> Into black, bony masks. Before we knew
> We're into them . . . "Swine!"—"Die then!"—"That's for you!"[8]

Also,

> I saw an old, old man
> Lying before my feet with shattered skull
> And both my arms dripped red.[9]

The influence of his war memories seems obvious. Images of hand-to-hand combat in no man's land, the unmistakable reference to gas masks, as well as dismemberment, and the German shouts as the battle rages are clear references to World War I trench warfare. In fact, apart from a few letters, these may be the most explicit revelations of Lewis's recollections of the war.

There is more. Having left this man, Dymer travels on and finally sleeps out in the open when, "suddenly, from dreaming / He woke wide into present horror, screaming."[10] He was dreaming of the arms of his beloved when the dream suddenly turns into a nightmare and was

> filled with night alarms
> And rapping guns: and men with splintered faces,

---

[7]Lewis, *Dymer,* IV.26.
[8]Lewis, *Dymer,* IV.27.
[9]Lewis, *Dymer,* IV.28.
[10]Lewis, *Dymer,* V.5.

—No eyes, no nose, all red—were running races
With worms along the floor.[11]

Here a reader can easily imagine that when the battles were long behind him Lewis's memories still haunted his sleep. The memories of war appear to linger, influencing what he writes so vividly in *Dymer*.

The implicit influence of myth. Another implicit influence on this narrative poem was Lewis's abiding interest in mythology. He makes only slight reference to myth in the 1950 preface, yet he does say much about his love of myth in the letters he wrote while composing *Dymer*. Furthermore, he reveals his early fascination with myth in his autobiography. The flavor of myth is pervasive in the poem because the lifelong love of myth was pervasive in Lewis throughout his life.

Surprised by Joy *and Lewis's early love of myth.* In *Surprised by Joy* Lewis told the story of his pilgrimage from atheism to Christianity.[12] He recalls that in his earliest days a longing was awakening in him but the object of this longing was not clear. Various things called to his interior life: beauty, nature, the quality that met him in the books he was reading, and so forth. However, one of the things that fed this longing was an emerging interest in myth generally, and Norse mythology most of all. In his autobiography, he writes that these Norse myths became for him more important than anything else.[13] They focused his longing on stories that suggested the transcendent and supernatural. This aroma is also pervasive in *Dymer*.

Lewis chronicles the coupling of this longing with the myths and the part they played in nudging him toward whatever object might satisfy them. Consequently, Lewis was interested in much that was mythological. Also during this time in his life, he picked up interest in Wagner's musical depictions of these stories. He never forgot the day when he walked into the Belfast shop of T. Edens Osborne and heard the *Ride*

---

[11]Lewis, *Dymer*, V.6.
[12]C. S. Lewis, *Surprised by Joy: The Shape of My Early Life* (New York: Harcourt, Brace and Company, 1956), vii.
[13]Lewis, *Surprised by Joy*, 76.

of the Valkyries playing. The event fed his passion for the music depicting that world. He spent all his pocket money to buy recordings of the *Ring*, and *Lohengrin*, and *Parsifal*.[14] Lewis notes that the myths did something else for him as well.

> If Northerness seemed then a bigger thing than my religion, that may partly have been because my attitude toward it contained elements which my religion ought to have contained and did not. It was not itself a new religion, for it contained no trace of belief and imposed no duties. Yet unless I am greatly mistaken there was in it something very like adoration, some kind of disinterested self-abandonment to an object which sincerely claimed this by simply being the object it was. Sometimes I can almost think that I was sent back to the false gods there to acquire some capacity for worship against the day when the true God should recall me to Himself. Not that I might not have learned this sooner and more safely in ways I shall now never know without apostasy, but that Divine punishments are also mercies, and particular good is worked out of particular evil, and penal blindness made sanative.[15]

Definition of myth. At this time, Lewis understood myth to be a story that has a quality about it where the words or the medium of communication are less significant than the story itself. In fact, the story can be communicated many ways. The Greek word *muthos* simply means story; but these stories, as Lewis understood them, work "upon us by [their] particular flavor or quality, rather as a smell or chord does."[16] He adds that the story may be sad or joyful, but it is always grave. The reason for the gravity is that the story is felt to be numinous, transcendent, awe-inspiring, "as if something of great moment has been communicated to us."[17] In this

[14]Lewis, *Surprised by Joy*, 74-75.
[15]Lewis, *Surprised by Joy*, 76-77.
[16]C. S. Lewis, *An Experiment in Criticism* (Cambridge: Cambridge University Press, 1961), 43.
[17]Lewis, *Experiment in Criticism*, 44.

sense, Lewis says that a myth is "extra literary."[18] I think he is attempting to depict this in *Dymer*.

Myth and meaning. Benjamin Jowett, the eminent English translator of Plato, says that philosophy was born out of the myths. They were attempts to explain by means of story the significance of observed natural phenomena. Sometimes conflicting accounts came to be, and these, in turn, led to critical thinking as the ancients debated the relative merits of contrasting myths. It was an attempt to make sense of one's experience and understand one's place in the world.[19] Therefore, myths were a quest for meaning. This was certainly so for Lewis; myth gave him a vehicle by which he sought to make sense of his own longings, seeking to understand what they might mean and to direct his search for their proper object.[20] It is only natural to suppose that as Lewis wrote *Dymer*, his pleasure in myth-making, or *mythopoeia*, as he called it, and his sense of longing would have an influence on the poem.

Dymer *and the flavor of myth.* Lewis is able to summarize the myth of *Dymer* simply enough.

> My hero was to be a man escaping from illusion. He begins by egregiously supposing the universe to be his friend and seems for a time to find confirmation of his belief. Then he tries, as we all try, to repeat his moment of youthful rapture. It cannot be done; the old Matriarch sees to that. On top of his rebuff comes the discovery of the consequences which his rebellion against the City has produced. He sinks into despair and gives utterance to the pessimism which had, on the whole, been my own view about six years earlier. Hunger and a shock of real danger bring him to his senses and he at last accepts reality. But just as he is setting out on the new and soberer life, the shabbiest of all brides is offered him; the false promise that by magic or invited illusion there may be a short cut back to the one happiness he

---

[18]Lewis, *Experiment in Criticism*, 42.

[19]Benjamin Jowett, *Selected Passages from Plato's Introductions* (London: John Murray, 1902), 16-19, 167-72.

[20]More will be discussed about this theme later.

remembers. He relapses and swallows the bait, but he has grown too mature to be really deceived. He finds that the wish-fulfillment dream leads to the fear-fulfillment dream, recovers himself, defies the Magician who tempted him, and faces his destiny.[21]

At the time he was writing *Dymer*, Lewis was rereading the *Hippolytus* by Euripides.[22] In *Surprised by Joy*, he says this occurred at a time when God was closing in on him. Inspired by Euripides, Lewis writes, "I was once more into the land of longing."[23] Furthermore, this Greek myth was one of several things that triggered his coming to faith. In this regard, *Dymer* takes on even more significance.

As Euripides tells the story, Hippolytus was the son of Theseus and an Amazon. Aphrodite hates Hippolytus because he has pledged his allegiance to Artemis, her rival among the goddesses. Aphrodite casts a spell on Theseus's current wife, Phaedra, causing her to desire Hippolytus, her stepson. Aphrodite's intention is to stir Theseus to jealousy so he will destroy his own son. Phaedra struggles, caught between the spell to love Hippolytus and her desire to be faithful to her husband. Her nurse, detecting Phaedra's struggle, invites her to confide her secret. Phaedra confesses her love for Hippolytus. The nurse, seeking to broker a union between Phaedra and Hippolytus, lets the secret of Phaedra's love become a point of gossip and scandal. Unable to resolve the conflict within her and horrified at the false gossip about her, Phaedra takes her own life. When Theseus becomes aware of the gossip but not the actual truth, he rushes to judgment and banishes his son, Hippolytus. Theseus's judgment is both uninformed and cruel. Consequently, Hippolytus suffers unduly because of his father's cruelties. Artemis appears to tell Theseus that he made judgments without full understanding. Theseus is beside himself with the loss of his wife, and now his son is dying. Nevertheless, before

---

[21]Preface, 13-14.

[22]C. S. Lewis, *All My Road Before Me: The Diary of C. S. Lewis 1922–1927*, ed. Walter Hooper (San Diego: Harcourt Brace Jovanovich, 1991), 296, 299.

[23]Lewis, *Surprised by Joy*, 217.

he dies, Hippolytus is carried to his father and in his presence forgives his father as he dies. Theseus is overwhelmed by this willingness of his son to forgive him in the very hour of his death.

The play ends with the chorus singing: "On all our citizens hath come this universal sorrow, unforeseen. Now shall the copious tear gush forth, for sad news about great men takes more than unusual hold upon the heart."[24] In fact, no less than five of Euripides's plays end with words very similar to the sentiments of the *Hippolytus*: "Many are the shapes that fortune takes, and oft the gods bring things to pass beyond our expectation. That which we deemed so sure is not fulfilled, while for that we never thought would be, God finds out a way. And such hath been the issue in the present case."[25]

What significance does this have when it comes to Lewis's *Dymer*? The message throughout is that "reality is iconoclastic." In addition, *Hippolytus* underscores another feature of the influence of myth on Lewis. His early letters show he had no real interest in Euripides.[26] However, something changed in him. Later, by his own admission, the story of *Hippolytus* affects his own writing and in fact becomes the inspiration at the root of another of his narrative poems, "The Queen of the Drum."[27] On March 4, 1924, Lewis writes in his journal, at the very time he is writing *Dymer*, that *Hippolytus* is "splendid stuff."[28] And, as has been mentioned, just before his conversion to Christianity, the "first move" in the process where God puts him in "checkmate" was the reading of *Hippolytus*. There are several very important things to note here in relation to *Dymer*. Just as the characters in Euripides's play must accept their fate, so too, as Lewis mentions in his 1950 preface, "[My hero] at last accepts reality."[29] This stoicism is also noticeable in *Dymer's* accepting his fate and resigning himself to reality.

---

[24]Euripides, *The Plays of Euripides*, trans. Edward P. Coleridge, vol. 5, *Great Books of the Western World* (Chicago: Encyclopedia Britannica, 1952), 236.

[25]Euripides, *The Plays of Euripides; Alcestis*, 247; *Medea*, 224; *Helen*, 314; *Bacchantes*, 352; and *Andromache*, 326.

[26]Lewis, *Collected Letters*, 1:408.

[27]Lewis, *Collected Letters*, 1:466.

[28]Lewis, *All My Road Before* Me, 296.

[29]Preface, 14.

These tributaries coming from the springs of Euripides feed into the stream of Lewis's growing commitment to the idea that "reality is iconoclastic." It is because Lewis held this vision of reality that in time he was able to move away from his early atheism back to God as the object of his deepest longing. Since evidence of this move can be traced in *Dymer*, the poem is once again an important literary artifact chronicling Lewis's progress toward an eventual conversion to Christianity.

The Nordic myths and Dymer: *the waking of desire.* Lewis wrote to Greeves as he was revising *Dymer* and said that "'Dymer' is changed to 'Ask' (you remember Ask and Embla in the Norse myths)?" He was also thinking of changing the title to "The Redemption of Ask."[30] Ask and Embla were equivalent to Adam and Eve in the Nordic myths. The association of *Dymer* with Nordic mythology is made explicit here. Lewis makes more connections between *Dymer* and the Norse myths in the same letter and recounts the late night talk he had with Hugo Dyson and J. R. R. Tolkien shortly before his conversion.

> Now what Dyson and Tolkien showed me was that if I met the idea of sacrifice in a Pagan story I didn't mind it at all: again, that if I met the idea of a god sacrificing himself to himself (cf. the quotation opposite the title page of *Dymer*) I liked it very much and was mysteriously moved by it: again, the idea of the dying and reviving god (like Balder, Adonis, Bacchus) similarly moved me provided I met it anywhere except in the Gospels."[31]

Lewis put these lines from the *Hàvamàl*, a collection of Icelandic poems, opposite the title page of *Dymer*: "Nine nights I hung upon the Tree, wounded with the spear as an offering to Odin, myself sacrificed to myself." This reference also connects *Dymer* to the Nordic sagas.

The avian portent is another indicator of the influence of Norse mythology on *Dymer*. In the sagas, Odin, the chief god of the pantheon, has

---

[30]Lewis, *Collected Letters*, 1:419.
[31]Lewis, *Collected Letters*, 976-77.

two ravens, Huginn, whose name meant "thought," and Muninn, whose name meant "memory." These two birds fly all about the various kingdoms and report to Odin what has occurred in that world. These birds do not give omniscience to Odin but they widen his vision of the world and often enough give a kind of suggestion as to what is ahead. This use of birds to indicate what is coming is not an unusual device in literature. Chaucer and Shakespeare often use the song or call of birds—particularly larks, cuckoos, crows, or vultures—to indicate what is ahead. Lewis uses this device in *Dymer*. One cannot read the poem without noticing the presence of birds and the frequency with which they signal what is to come. Birds guide Dymer out of the City and into nature. Foreboding events are signaled by the flight of crows. In all, there are thirty-one references to birds in the poem, and in most cases, they are portents. One particular negative example occurs when Dymer witnesses the shooting of a singing lark. This happens just before he comes to the house of the magician. On his arrival, the magician asks,

> 'Have you heard
> My gun? It was but now I killed a lark.'
> 'What, Sir!' said Dymer; 'shoot the singing bird?'
> 'Sir,' said the man, 'they sing from dawn till dark,
> And interrupt my dreams.'[32]

This telegraphs what is coming. Dymer was sufficiently warned that nothing good was likely to occur at the magician's house. This is also a foreshadowing of what is ahead in much of Lewis's writing. Virtually all of his evil characters are cruel to animals. Furthermore, this cruelty grows to become a cruelty toward humans as well. Nevertheless, for our purposes here, it is only important to note this further indicator that the Norse myths had an influence on Lewis as he wrote *Dymer*.

The idea of myth as a literary form by which Lewis connects his love of myth and his interest in the idea of longing is in evidence in *Dymer*.

---

[32]Lewis, *Dymer*, VI.10.

There will be more to say about the nature of longing, but we must first move from implicit influences to those that Lewis explicitly identifies in his 1950 preface.

EXPLICIT INFLUENCES ON *DYMER*

Lewis identifies at least four concepts that influenced his writing of *Dymer*. These are: the idea of *escape*; his rejection of *Christina Dreams*; his doubts about the *new psychology*; and his interest in the *longings* that stirred in him, and still troubled him, since childhood.

Escape. Lewis wrote, "My hero was to be a man escaping from illusion."[33] Lewis's hero is "a" man. Dymer is a particular man, not a mere abstraction or a "universal" man, or an "everyman." In a letter written to his brother nearly contemporaneously to the publication of *Dymer*, Lewis acknowledged that though abstractions and generalizations have their positive use they can also become distractions. He notes where they are likely to go amiss:

> the 18th century was fond of personifying abstractions ("Corruption had seized the provinces" etc.) and because Carlyle carried that further and gave a tinge of poetry in his French Revolution, whence it passed into every writer who wants to write impressively on political and historical subjects, we have now reached a stage at which causes, movements, tendencies etc. are talked of as if they were real things who did things: as if it were Bolshevism, not Bolsheviks, who fomented revolutions, and the revolutionary spirit, instead of the revolutionary spirits, which made men drunk.[34]

It is not a particular Bolshevik with whom I may debate, but rather, as I make a pronouncement against all Bolsheviks, universalizing my claim I can leave out significant exceptions that might count against my judgments. Dymer is *a man*, escaping from illusions. One of the great illusions

---

[33]Preface, 13.
[34]Lewis, *Collected Letters*, 1:704.

of this, and perhaps any day, is to break free of the tyranny of wholesale categorizations. Nevertheless, categorizations have a rhetorical value, but they must be used cautiously.

What is the point of all of this and why is it relevant? Lewis scholar Bruce Edwards once observed to me, in conversation, that the academic enterprise consisted of seeing patterns and exceptions. If one never saw the patterns, no generalizations or abstractions necessary to pass on a body of knowledge could be made. That is the rhetorical value. On the other hand, without recognition of the exceptions the generalizations are always false. As Lewis observed, there is nothing in the history of thought like a shoreline in geography: one minute I am in the water, the next step I am on the sandy shore.[35] One minute I am studying the Middle Ages, the next I am studying the Renaissance. Furthermore, nobody was running around in the Middle Ages saying, "I live in the Middle Ages!" As Lewis rightly observed, periodization may be an academic necessity, on one level, but to the degree we fail to recognize we are doing it, we may unwittingly universalize judgments and thereby inflate our own estimation of a particular matter. Furthermore, to the degree we become emotionally involved in the use of abstractions, we can create assumptions by which we make judgments of others who do not see things as we see them. Taken in by such subjectivism, we fail to recognize complexities and exceptions that exist beyond our scope of things. Those who do not see matters as we see them, or as our party tends to see them, can be dismissed with a mere roll of the eyes. Lewis, when he is at his best, will not allow this to occur. He is not writing about "men," but a man. He is not making a universal judgment, but a particular one. Here is the life of one man, Dymer. Here are his circumstances, given his unique situation; this is how he responded, for good or for ill. As the poem unfolds, we see that his choices are full of consequences both good and bad—that is, they are fraught with the kinds of complexities that honest assessments would lead us to expect. We make no universal

---

[35]Lewis, *Selected Literary Essays*, 2-3.

judgments; we must wait and see what will happen. Furthermore, Dymer's story is complex, full of inflated assumptions and the consequences of erroneous judgments. A universal judgment that his acts were bad would vilify those elements in Dymer's choices that were good; and a universal judgment of good would tend to overlook the bad. Dymer is a man escaping from illusion; those who read this poem closely may benefit from the fact that this is so.

In some ways, Lewis's approach to *Dymer*, and his conscious awareness of the problems of abstraction, has much to say to us today, where our own cultural and political dismissiveness of others has led to great incivility. We do not listen; we just assume we have fully grasped both our position and that of others. We self-referentially prejudge situations beyond merit, justifying, in our minds, our own prejudices while calling out what we perceive to be the prejudices of others. We cannot hear nor believe there might be nuances in the positions of others that would make them seem reasonable. We already know what is wrong with their party, so we do not have to listen any longer. Dymer is "a" man. He is not the "universal" man. His is not "everyman"; he is a particular man, in an imagined set of circumstances, and we get to wander into his story, to see and experience what he saw and endured given the framework and limitations of this story. When this works best, it is possible for us to see in a world such as Dymer's the kinds of things we even experience in our own world.

Again, we are told that Dymer is a man escaping. From what is he escaping? Certainly, there are many examples of escape in Dymer. He escapes from the City. He escapes from the castle and then cannot reenter. He escapes from the magician's house and his spells. He must even escape from false notions of himself. In describing Dymer's escape from the city, Lewis writes that he goes "beyond the wall."[36] The idea of a hero escaping "beyond the wall" occurs often in Lewis, for instance in *Spirits in Bondage*, Lewis's first book, and published before *Dymer*, Lewis wrote,

---

[36]Lewis, *Dymer*, I.13.

I catch a sight of lands beyond the wall,
I see a strange god's face.
And some day this will work upon me so.
I shall arise and leave both friends and home
And over many lands a pilgrim go
Through alien woods and foam,
Seeking the last steep edges of the earth
Whence I may leap into that gulf of light
Wherein, before my narrowing Self had birth,
Part of me lived aright.[37]

The escape from some boundary, in order to find an object that would fulfill a mysterious, deep-seated desire, is in evidence in much of Lewis's fiction. This is an early expression of that. Furthermore, Lewis explains that *Dymer* seeks to capture the "extreme" anarchism that characterized much of the world when he first penned the story.[38] Nevertheless, Dymer's bolt from the City was not rooted in a self-referential anarchy but in a quest to leave the contrived, and unreal, to find the real. Dymer is a man not merely fleeing a City but also fleeing a false notion of the world around him, perhaps even a false notion of himself. In other words, Dymer is a man escaping from illusion. Lewis writes much about the idea of escape as a concept in literature; this is seen in works of nonfiction like *An Experiment in Criticism*, or *Of Other Worlds*. However, Lewis also plays with the concept of escape in his fiction: *The Great Divorce*, *That Hideous Strength*, *The Horse and His Boy*, and *Till We Have Faces* come immediately to mind. One thing is apparent to the reader: Lewis's interest in a man escaping from illusion is another depiction of "reality is iconoclastic."

---

[37]C. S. Lewis, *Spirits in Bondage: A Cycle of Lyrics* (London: William Heinemann, 1919), 86-87. It is also interesting to note Lewis's use of contrast between "white roads" leading out to a wider world, "Where the gods unseen in their valleys green are glad at the ends of earth / And fear no morrow to bring them sorrow, nor night to quench their mirth," 92. Similar images of escape from restricted, cloistered environments into a world more real and distant are scattered throughout *Spirits in Bondage*.

[38]Preface, 10.

Christina Dreams. When Lewis warns against the "Christina Dream," what did he mean? Something of his concern is expressed as he discusses his own experiences as a student:

> In those days the new psychology was just beginning to make itself felt in the circles I most frequented at Oxford. This joined forces with the fact that we felt ourselves (as young men always do) to be escaping from the illusions of adolescence, and as a result we were much exercised about the problem of fantasy or wishful thinking. The "Christina Dream," as we called it (after Christina Pontifex in Butler's novel), was the hidden enemy whom we were all determined to unmask and defeat. My hero, therefore, had to be a man who had succumbed to its allurements and finally got the better of them.[39]

Later in the 1950 preface Lewis adds, "By the time I wrote *Dymer* I had come, under the influence of our common obsession about Christina Dreams, into a state of angry revolt against that spell. I regarded it as the very type of the illusions I was trying to escape from."[40]

First let me bring definition to the Christina Dream. Lewis's former student, longtime friend, and biographer, George Sayer, claims that the "main subject of *Dymer* . . . is without doubt the temptation of fantasies,"[41] and these fantasies are what Lewis calls "Christina Dreams."[42] Sayer asserts that these dreams speak of the awakening of sexual desire and the fantasies of adolescence; they are about sexual interest and attraction. Furthermore, he says that *Dymer* was written by Lewis in "a state of angry revolt against that spell."[43] I think Sayer is wrong in his assessment. First, Lewis wrote the poem over nearly a decade. It is hard to imagine he sustained a state of angry revolt for such a long spell. Second, the "Christina Dream" is not inherently a sexual fantasy at all. Some familiarity with Samuel Butler's

---

[39]Preface, 11.
[40]Preface, 11-12.
[41]Sayer, "C. S. Lewis's *Dymer*," 11.
[42]Preface, 11. Also Sayer, "C. S. Lewis's *Dymer*," 97.
[43]Sayer, "C. S. Lewis's *Dymer*," 97.

novel will correct the misunderstanding, which is important to do if one is to grasp Lewis's point properly and interpret the poem accurately.

Butler's Christina Pontifex is not a person to arouse the libido. In fact, she is simply a rather uninteresting and compliant character. When the reader first meets her, she appears manipulative as she connives ways to get Theobald Pontifex to marry her. Theobald is not the most desirable of men. He is not even a man her parents are very fond of, but "a bird in the hand is worth two in the bush." She prefers marriage to anyone readily available rather than the single life. Christina is older than Theobald and, recognizing her prospects for marriage are diminishing, plays a round of poker with her four unmarried sisters for the unrivaled position of seeking the hand of the new assistant to her pastor-father. She cultivates what Butler calls "the Mammon of Righteousness." If she walks circumspectly and plays her part well—that is, if she practices "righteousness" before the young pastoral intern—she may win the rewards of "righteousness." Her route in this regard is one of compliance.[44] Nevertheless, once she has landed her husband she nearly loses her identity by constantly caving in to the rigid and rather unreasonable Theobald. Christina is anything but an object of sexual desire. Simply put, she is not even an accurate representation of a woman. She has lost her identity, becoming utterly complacent to the wishes of the man who becomes her husband.

Furthermore, whenever there seems to be a conflict of interest between Christina and her husband, she is always deferential. In this way, Christina Pontifex represents a false notion of reality and a false notion of women. One should not expect another human being to be so malleable to the wishes of others. This is the "Christina Dream," to see others as a mere extension of one's own projection. Several examples from Butler's novel demonstrate the point. First, prior to her engagement, throughout the betrothal period, and even after marriage, Christina suppresses her wishes and desires to the interests of her husband. Second, after their marriage,

---

[44]Samuel Butler, *The Way of All Flesh* (Mineola, NY: Dover Publications, 2004), 41.

on the first night of their honeymoon, a conflict arises and Theobald makes it clear that "he was master now." Christina, losing her way in the conflict, yields to his thoughtless demands, and begs his forgiveness for failing to obey him, acknowledging that, of course, he is right.[45] Their honeymoon was little more than a wife-training school, a sort of marital boot camp. In fact, Butler notes, "The end of the Honeymoon saw Mrs. Theobald the most devotedly obsequious wife in all England."[46] Third, in times of difficulty, outside the home and in the parish where Theobald comes to pastor, Christina sees her role in life as little more than to admire him publicly, await him whenever he is away from home, and assure him whenever he returns.[47] "Her principal duty was, as she well said, to her husband—to love him, honor him, and keep him in good temper."[48] Fourth, Butler observes,

> Oh what a comfort it was to Theobald to reflect that he had a wife on whom he could rely never to cost him a sixpence of unauthorized expenditure! Letting alone her absolute submission, the perfect co-incidence of her opinion with his own on every subject and her constant assurances to him that he was right in everything which he took in his head to say or to do, what a tower of strength to him was her exactness in money matters! As years went by he became as fond of his wife as it was in his nature to be of any living thing, and applauded himself for having stuck to his engagement—a piece of virtue of which he was now reaping the reward.[49]

To read Butler is to remove all ambiguity of what Lewis meant about "Christina Dreams." These dreams were all self-referential and utilitarian. Theobald Pontifex loses all touch with reality when he becomes the center of his world. Others matter, if, and only if, they matter to him. Lewis's

---

[45]Butler, *The Way of All Flesh*, 44-45.
[46]Butler, *The Way of All Flesh*, 46.
[47]Butler, *The Way of All Flesh*, 51.
[48]Butler, *The Way of All Flesh*, 53.
[49]Butler, *The Way of All Flesh*, 54.

concern is to show, in *Dymer*, that reality is not at all like the Christina Dream, because "reality is iconoclastic." Facing the world as it is, Dymer must break free of his false notions and projections. He must, as Lewis says, face reality.

Further clarity about the Christina Dream can be found by looking ahead to what Lewis wrote of Butler's novel in *The Four Loves*. He says there is a perversion of family affection that tyrannizes by the need to be needed. It is controlling and solicitous. When looking for literary characters to make his point, he draws on the character Theobald Pontifex, and writes, "The egregious Mr. Pontifex in *The Way of All Flesh* is outraged to discover that his son does not love him; it is 'unnatural' for a boy not to love his own father. It never occurs to him to ask whether, since the first day the boy can remember, he has ever done or said anything that could excite love."[50] Theobald boxes in his son, as well as Christina. He coerces both of them to be nothing more than extensions of his warped imagination. Christina does not represent reality at all. Lewis came to realize that his imagined, adolescent view of women, fed by the Butler character, was not at all accurate. Theobald, in the novel, is the culprit. Borrowing from Charles Williams, Theobald experiences his own "descent into hell," and Christina Dreams enable him to do this. The problem would occur to anyone who failed to see the complexities of the real world, choosing only to believe in one's own projections. Robert Browning in his poem "Rabbi Ben Ezra" says, "Then welcome each rebuff that turns earth's smoothness rough."[51] Welcome those complexities that help you to see the world as it truly is, rather than how you would have it be. Lewis was beginning to value a "reality is iconoclastic" approach to life, and Christina Dreams were antithetical to that value. Reality is not at all as Butler portrays this woman. Lewis would write much later in his career, "In coming to understand anything we must reject the facts as they are for us in favor of the facts as they are."[52]

---

[50]C. S. Lewis, *The Four Loves* (New York: Harcourt, Brace & World, 1960), 62-63.

[51]Robert Browning, "Rabbi Ben Ezra," in *British Poets of the Nineteenth Century*, ed. Curtis Hidden Page (Boston: Benjamin H. Sanborn, 1904), 659.

[52]Lewis, *Experiment in Criticism*, 138.

A careless reading of *Dymer* might lead one to think the "Christina Dream" was an allusion to some sort of sexual fantasy, especially since Dymer temporarily falls to the temptation of the salacious dreams the magician seeks to foster on him. The "dream," the approach to reality that is self-projective rather than self-aware, will certainly make one susceptible to any number of temptations, but the Christina Dream itself is not a sexual fantasy. Dymer has been on a quest to find the woman he abandoned in the castle. Nevertheless, it is a mistake to believe Dymer's sole motivation is to find sexual satisfaction. In fact, Dymer's interest in finding the woman once again is for something much deeper. He wants to escape his own cowardice. Furthermore, he wants to find the woman as she truly is, and that is more than what he projected on her during their tryst in the castle. He realized how shabby he had been after leaving the castle, and that he did not even know her name. He regretted that he used her. Lewis's rhetorical interests lie elsewhere.

Dymer, in his quest to escape from illusion, longs for the real wherever it may lead him. Yet, in his pilgrimage, in Cantos VI and VII, he comes upon the magician who seeks to draw him back into the veil of illusion and the world of dreams. The magician's home, and all about it, was built to block out any reminder of the real world. A hedge surrounds it and hides all traces of the world beyond. There is a clock tower, but the clock is broken and no indications of real time interrupt the falsity of the world the magician has created for himself. The magician announces to Dymer shortly after they meet that he was the one who killed the lark; his motive: they interrupt his dreams. He will have nothing of the real world that he might remain in the fiction of his own making. It is in the presence of this magician that one could gain the impression that the Christina Dream had a sexual connotation. This is because here Lewis connects the Christina projection with the "new psychology." He is showing that a dominating subjectivity can lead to any amount of evil.

The new psychology. This new psychology, as Lewis saw it, interpreted the actions of others as the desire to fulfill wishes and experience pleasure, or the avoidance of fear-fulfillments in an attempt to escape pain. This new psychology was rooted in Freudian thought and, as Lewis depicted it, sought to find underlying causes for everything. In *Dymer*, Lewis's magician embodies the abuses of the new psychology.

Lewis writes of this new psychology in *Surprised by Joy*. Drawing from Lewis's autobiography it is possible to refine what Lewis meant when he wrote of the new psychology.

> The new Psychology was at that time sweeping through us all. We did not swallow it whole (few people then did) but we were all influenced. What we were most concerned about was "Fantasy" or wishful thinking." For (of course) we were all poets and critics and set a very high value on "Imagination" in some high Coleridgean sense, so it became important to distinguish Imagination, not only (as Coleridge did) from Fancy, but also from Fantasy as the psychologists understood that term. Now what, I asked myself, were all my delectable mountains and western gardens but sheer Fantasies? Had they not revealed their true nature by luring me, time and time again, into undisguisedly erotic reverie or the squalid nightmare of Magic?[53]

Lewis's connecting the new psychology to magic is not wasted on those who read *Dymer*. The longings awakened in Lewis as a child seemed to evaporate as he became an atheist and materialist. He could explain them all away as mere wish-fulfillment dreams. For a time he suppressed the very desire in him which was awakened by the vivid scenes of nature that he loved; these were only mere fantasies, wish-fulfillment dreams. These things were explained away as having been caused by the disappointments of his childhood, the early death of his mother, the estrangement he felt from his father, or the disappointments he experienced at school. On the other hand, the deep desire and the longings he so often felt, he decided were not real. This new psychology took him in, but only briefly, with its "wishful thinking" providing his imagination with whatever he wanted. By

---

[53]Lewis, *Surprised by Joy*, 203-4.

the time Lewis wrote *Dymer*, however, he was strongly second-guessing the new psychology, and the longings were again finding quarter in his heart and mind. He began, once again, to suspect that they might actually be for some real, not merely imagined, object. Therefore, he wrote in the 1950 preface, "My hero, therefore, had to be a man who had succumbed to its allurements and finally got the better of them. But the particular form in which this was worked out depended on two peculiarities of my own history."[54] These two peculiarities were the "Christina Dream," that false notion of reality, and the deep longings he was beginning to rediscover as indicators of the substantially real and transcendent. It is time to turn attention to the longings.

Longing. Again, in his autobiography, as well as his 1950 preface, Lewis linked the myths with a stirring up of a sense of deep longing within him. I want to turn attention to the kinds and qualities of these longings. Lewis's desire, and in some ways the preoccupation of his early life, was to find the object of his longing. Dymer, too, is questing to find something, but the object is never completely clear. Lewis writes *Dymer* as he is closing in on the day when he would discover God as the object of these deep-seated desires. In fact, his conversion would follow only five years after the publication of *Dymer*. In virtually all of his books, Lewis gives indication of these longings. *Dymer* in this regard is not unique.

Lewis's *The Pilgrim's Regress: An Allegorical Apology for Christianity, Reason, and Romanticism* was the first book he published after *Dymer*. This was his first explicitly Christian book, and he wrote the first draft only a year after his conversion, over a period of a few weeks, this while vacationing in the Belfast home of his friend Arthur Greeves. This is Lewis's only allegory, and the hero, John, is also on a quest to escape from illusions. He is living in a town called Puritania, in some ways not unlike Dymer's City. He sees a vision of an island, and it awakens in his heart a longing to find the island. John must also break free and go beyond a wall to begin his pilgrim quest

---

[54]Preface, 11.

for this object of his desire. Ultimately, he seeks to find that which can unite both his reason and the romantic longings of his heart. In his travels, John comes to a hermit who, in the allegory, represents history. The hermit refers to God as "the Landlord." In addition, the hermit says, "The Landlord succeeded in getting a lot of messages through."[55] By these messages, Lewis refers to the myths in pagan times, or stories from other times. The hermit says that these stories were one of the means by which the world awakens to long for God.

The hermit speaks of three primary kinds of myth and the specific periods in history when the particular flavor of longing was most developed. First, during pagan times: longing for a place "east or west of the world" was developed in the pilgrim literature of classical times. It is the longing depicted by Homer's *The Odyssey* in which Ulysses desires to return to his beloved Penelope at his home in Ithaca. Virgil also writes of it in the *Aeneid*, where the hero of the story is caught between Troy, the city of his birth, and Rome, the city that will one day be. This is a longing for place. One could say it is a heaven longing.[56] In *Dymer*, Lewis depicts something like this longing when his hero sees the real world from the window of the lecture hall in his City and bolts from the artificial to quest for the real. It is also seen in the made-up world of the magician and Dymer's willingness, at all costs, to break free from the illusions to that which is substantive.

Second, the hermit says during Medium Aevum (or Middle Ages), the longing was awakened by a picture or image of a lady. The reference is to Dante and the image of Beatrice,[57] but it is also suggested by Guillaume de Lorris's *The Romance of the Rose* and perhaps again in Chaucer's *Troilus and Cressida*. Lewis depicts a similar longing in *Dymer*. It is first manifest when Dymer has his tryst with the real woman in the castle. This inspires his pilgrimage to seek for her. In a manner not unlike Dante, Dymer discovers

---

[55]C. S. Lewis, *The Pilgrim's Regress: An Allegorical Apology for Christianity, Reason, and Romanticism* (London: Geoffrey Bles, 1945), 153.
[56]Lewis, *The Pilgrim's Regress*, 157.
[57]Lewis, *The Pilgrim's Regress*, 157-58.

the longing for the lady is ultimately a longing for God. After leaving the magician's house, wounded and broken, he encounters his lady. He discovers that she is a goddess and that somehow God has prompted all of his questing. The Lewis of *Dymer* has none of the assurances the mature Lewis would find. His Dymer asks the goddess,

> "Give me the truth! I ask not now for pity.
> When gods call, can the following them be sin?
> Was it false light that lured me from the City?
> Where was the path—without it or within? . . .
> Has heaven no voice to help? Must things of dust
> Guess their own way in the dark?" She said, "They must."[58]

Then Dymer cries in wrath, saying, "You came in human shape, in sweet disguise / Wooing me, lurking for me in my path." He says, in anguish, "All was lies." The goddess answers, "For our kind must come to all / If bidden, but in the shape for which they call."[59] Dymer discovers what Dante discovered, and ironically, Lewis had yet to discover.

Third, in the Romantic era the hermit says the longing was awakened by landscapes and nature.[60] The images are depicted in works like Wordsworth's *The Prelude* and other Romantic poets. These poets recognized, on the threshold of the industrial age, the spoiling of nature and more. The polluting without was only a symptom of pollution within. The poets longed to return to the pure, the unspoiled, and the lost innocence of youth. They sought a return to that which might restore the soul; nature was believed to be the object of their longing. Lewis captures something of this in the poem. Dymer finds a kind of temporary refreshment for his soul once he has gotten beyond the walls of the City and is out in the open spaces. He finds it again after his disappointments at the castle. Again, he takes solace in nature after witnessing the complaints and the death of the wounded man.

---

[58]Lewis, *Dymer*, VIII.12.
[59]Lewis, *Dymer*, VIII.13.
[60]Lewis, *The Pilgrim's Regress*, 159.

But none of it ultimately satisfies. In Canto V, Dymer experiences one of his brief periods of rest and recovery in nature, but it does not hold him for long. He suddenly begins to vent his anger and contempt at the god of nature. This, too, sounds similar to Lewis's own story. As this canto begins, all he has seen and heard dumbfound Dymer. He rushes further into the wood in an attempt to run from the horrors of the dead man he left behind. However, he does not gain any kind of permanent solace for his grief, even from nature. Within him is triggered a long complaint against the gods, which continues for nearly one third of the canto. The complaint is consistent with the kind of anger Lewis himself claims to have had around the time of the poem's composition, a time of pre-Christian angst directed at God. Dymer's cry at the end of his long complaint is "Great God, take back your world."[61] Dymer is the one, the reader has learned, who tends to misjudge matters. He is a man who frequently needs to be undeceived. His life is in process of constant accommodation to reality. In addition, it is a curious feature of the narrative that the complaint, unlike those found in other myths, is here against *God* and not *the gods*. Perhaps there is evidence here that the author has not properly distanced himself from his protagonist. This incongruity cannot be ignored. Dymer finds rest in nature, yet complains against the God of nature. He longs for rest, but cannot quiet the nightmare within. Here, we see evidence of this third type of longing, Dymer's desire to have the brokenness within fixed and restored.

There is no redemption in *Dymer*. Nevertheless, the protagonist accepts his destiny that he must yield his life to set right the things he has done. Once he has died in a brief battle with the monster who was his own offspring, all of nature reawakens and is restored. Of course, this is nothing like the Christianity Lewis would come to accept; nevertheless, it depicts the longing to have the broken and wounded mended and healed.

Interestingly, Evelyn Underhill also wrote of these three longings. I quote her here to show that others have detected the same longings, and

---

[61]Lewis, *The Pilgrim's Regress*, 50.

also because she writes of them with better clarity than the unconverted Lewis could depict them. Underhill says,

> There are three deep cravings of the self, three great expressions of man's restlessness which only mystic truth can fully satisfy. The first is a craving that makes him a pilgrim and a wanderer. It is the longing to go out from his normal world in search of a lost home and a better country. The next is that craving of heart for heart, the soul for his perfect mate which makes him a lover. And the third is the craving for inward purity and perfection which makes him an ascetic and at last resort a saint.[62]

These longings were among the explicit influences Lewis identified as he wrote *Dymer*.

FINAL THOUGHTS

Let me say it again, *Dymer* is an important literary artifact that reveals much about Lewis as a writer. In this chapter, we have seen once again development of the theme that "reality is iconoclastic." Furthermore, we have looked at those influences on Lewis as he wrote, both implicit and explicit, that which was "brooding alone beneath the strength of things." These are the streams that fed the river from which Lewis drew as he created *Dymer*. The next chapter will look at what is in germ in *Dymer* that comes to full flower in Lewis's later work.

---

[62]Evelyn Underhill, *Mysticism: A Study in the Nature and Development of Man's Spiritual Consciousness* (London: Methuen & C. Ltd., 1948), 126-27.

RESPONSE

Mark Lewis

It is with some measure of trepidation that I answer the call to respond to the paper offered by my dear friend of many years, Dr. Jerry Root, addressing the question of influences active in the mind and heart of C. S. Lewis as he created his epic poem *Dymer*, early on the way to becoming the writer that we all have come to know and many to revere. Dr. Root asks us to consider *Dymer* as a significant step along this path for Lewis, and suggests that by identifying and considering his influences we can make some inferences about his artistic footfalls—why the faint print in the snow happened here and not there. I have the unique opportunity to offer my thoughts in a room that is beautifully (some might even say *densely)* populated by friends and colleagues who, without many exceptions, know more about C. S. Lewis, and certainly more about literary scholarship, than I do. You can understand my trepidation!

My only hope, it seems, is to find my lane and stay in it. So what is my "lane"? What can I offer that might be useful to this discussion? You may be familiar with the 1981 German film *Mephisto*[1] in which Klaus Maria Brandauer plays an actor who comes to prominence in Nazi Germany through his growing complicity with Hitler's regime. In the film's powerful last scene, the actor is caught on the floor of Berlin's massive *stadion*, trying to flee the crosshairs of klieg lights, and in the final frames he looks directly into the camera and offers a one-line defense of his actions to the audience: "*Ich bin doch nur ein Schauspieler!*" or, "I am only an actor!"

---

[1] *Mephisto*, directed by István Szabó (London: Cinegate, 1981).

While the klieg lights image is admittedly a bit overstated, I do believe that if I have anything meaningful to offer in response to Dr. Root's words, we will all be served better if I stick to that claim—"*Ich bin doch nur ein Schauspieler!*" I am only an actor. What I know about this subject I do not know through the kind of passionate and meticulous research offered by Dr. Root, or by Dr. Jeffry Davis in his response to Dr. Root's first paper in this series. It is offered instead anecdotally and as a series of surmises about the artist's imagination, gained from forty years as a theater maker. So, for better or for worse, "*Ich bin doch nur ein Schauspieler.*"

Allow me to say right off the bat that I believe that what we are trying to consider and describe here—what might act as an influence on what an artist produces—seems to me to be at best a pretty imprecise exercise. In other words, trying to figure out *why* we make *what* we make, or even the *thing* we make, while useful in one sense, feels in other ways like a matter of simple conjecture. Works of art that are released into the world in the way a poem or a play is tend to stand or fall on their own, independent of the kind of defense provided by the explanations we few—"we happy few"—have considered. While we can certainly pursue this kind of discussion with some expectation of fruit, I also hope that we can agree that there is a part of meaning that lies exclusively in reception. Still, there is perhaps something significant to be gained by thinking about the "whys" inherent in this kind of discussion, and what kinds of things influence the artist's processes. Sometimes, artists do it themselves.

As a very young actor I had a rare opportunity to hear—in person—the great filmmaker Ingmar Bergman speak to a very small group of actors and theater makers. I wrote down something that Bergman said that evening in response to a question about his own way forward as a "maker." In other words, his process. He said, "I shoot an arrow into the dark. Then I follow that arrow. When I find it, I try to discern why it landed here, and not over there." (Then a pause, and a wry smile.) "It is a very boring process."

I think that in the preface to the second edition of *Dymer*, Lewis is trying to do a bit of the same thing. He is, in a sense, collecting his arrows. However, unlike Bergman in his "process" example, Lewis is doing so with a bit of antipathy and at a distance of almost twenty-five years. Furthermore, he is not doing so to plot a way forward, but rather to do some kind of clarifying work into writing that he feels quite distant from. He writes so that "[his] old poem might [not] be misunderstood by those who now read it for the first time." On the one hand, who can disagree that Lewis is generously assisting his readers, or trying to, with a few pieces of context? But I am of the opinion that when we make the kind of art that demands to be released into the world—a play or a poem or a film, for example—our efforts to keep readers or viewers from "misunderstanding" it are largely futile.

There are well-known examples in my discipline of great writers turning out plays whose own reception shocked them. Anton Chekhov famously accused Constantin Stanislavski of completely misunderstanding, and thereby ruining, the author's broad comedic intentions. (He produced them at his Moscow Art Theater in a groundbreaking acting style that included subtlety, subtext, and tragic consequences.) Similarly, Bertolt Brecht's "theater of alienation" demands that audiences *not* connect emotionally to characters like Mother Courage or Shen Te, "the good woman of Setzuan," because in doing so they make fuzzy the parts of the story that the author wants to make completely clear. Brecht's *alienation* style thereby forces the audience to acknowledge its own culpability in the story's events. The problem is that audiences cannot consistently manage to distance themselves from those stories in quite the way Brecht had hoped.

So, are we "misunderstanding" Chekhov? Brecht? Lewis in *Dymer*? Now, I want to make it clear that I think it's possible to *under*-understand. As I acknowledged a few moments ago, I am unwilling and underqualified to claim, in the same way that my colleague Jeff Davis did, why *Dymer* is perhaps simply not a very good poem. I seek to model here what I teach theater students: that to critique above the level you have achieved must be done with some awareness of just how difficult the process of creating something significant can be. In other words—you didn't like the actor playing Hamlet you just saw? Really? What was it like when *you* played it?

I have never written anything on the scale of an epic poem. I am not venturing, as some are actually qualified to do, to critique *Dymer*. But I am very willing to say that I was seldom compelled by it. And while I'm being confessional, I must offer here that Lewis's series of valid and illuminating points in the 1950 preface, offered so that we might not "misunderstand" his poem, was not an enormous help, as it presumes some measure of comfort in Plato, Wagner, *Siegfried*, the Hesperian or Western garden system, Euripides, Milton, Morris, the early Yeats (as well as the Yeats that Lewis visited in his occultist salon), Voltaire, Lucretius, Goethe, and Huxley (among others).

If there is any comfort for the rest of us, I believe it is that we *do* understand, or *don't* understand, or misunderstand, or even (horrors!) are profoundly bored by the nine cantos of *Dymer* for an entirely different set of reasons than is possible for Lewis to work out well in his preface.

I am ongoingly interested in the parameters of my own ability to connect not only intellectually but emotionally to things I read and see. Do you ever think about this? What is it that allows us to fully enter into a story being offered to us? What is it that opens me up in one moment of a story, and seems to shut me down in the next? I would like to offer a couple of thoughts on this.

First: Who is old enough to remember when car video players were still a recent phenomenon? We called ours "the silver bullet." We attempted to use it judiciously—mostly late in the day on long car trips. We had two daughters at the time, ages two and four, and they were absolutely mesmerized by it. The hypnotic effect seemed almost totally unrelated to content. It seemed to be the colorful dancing images alone that enthralled our children—and all without Benadryl! On one car trip to New York City, my wife and I popped a not-very-sophisticated animated version of *The Lion, the Witch and the Wardrobe* into the player; the images were not impressively drawn, and the visual effects felt a bit choppy. Nonetheless, Ruby, our two-year-old, went right to sleep (win!), and Olivia, our four-year-old, fell silent. Mary and I went about our business in the front of the car for quite some time when, suddenly, we heard a sound from the back seat that was absolutely unlike any we had ever heard our daughter make. It was a kind of wail. We looked back to discover Olivia hysterically laughing, while at the same time tears streamed down her face. And then came the words, "He's alive! Mama! Daddy! Aslan is not dead! He's not— he's *alive!*" Olivia was able to receive and understand, on a deep level, the very heart of Lewis's story. I would not have been capable of contextualizing it in a way that would have aided her understanding it at that level. It was, in a very real sense, a story *for* her.

Consider here Aslan's entrance into *The Lion, the Witch and the Wardrobe*. In George Sayer's account, it was only after Lewis had "written a good deal of the book, he got the idea of the lion Aslan, who 'came bounding into it.' Jack had been having a good many dreams of lions about that time . . . [and] once [Aslan] was there he pulled the whole story together, and soon he pulled the other six stories in after him."[2] Can you imagine Narnia without Aslan? For a long time, apparently, Lewis did.

On the other hand, I do not get a strong feeling when I read *Dymer* that the poem's main character ever meaningfully contradicts its very young author. In the sense that I believe Lewis intends it in his preface, his claims that the story simply "came to him" at the tender age of seventeen seems to me to be part of the problem with it. There is a kind of logic to the poem that does not allow for the kind of organic surprise a bounding lion provides. Maybe it takes some time to learn to trust and include dreams.

As early as Canto I, when Dymer whacks his professor for silencing his yawn and the poem simply moves past the event, we know we are in for a certain kind of experience, an experience where characters and events *symbolize* things and where it is quite possible to misunderstand (or misreceive) the meaning of the poem. The old vaudevillian adage proves true here: Man slips on a banana peel. What happens next tells us everything

---

[2]C. S. Lewis, "On Three Ways of Writing for Children," in *Of Other Worlds: Essays and Stories*, ed. Walter Hooper (London: Bles, 1966), quoted in George Sayer, *Jack: A Life of C. S. Lewis* (Wheaton, IL: Crossway, 1994), 312.

about the story we are experiencing. If the man pops up, we understand that we are in one kind of story. If he stays down and writhes in pain, we are in another kind. Dymer's actions early in the poem oddly do not invite us to take his epic journey with him. They seem *demonstrated* rather than lived through.

There is one quote in Lewis's *Dymer* preface that I immediately recognized —and it wasn't even cited! (I felt very accomplished . . .) "The heresies that men leave are hated most." Now, admittedly, the quote is from perhaps the world's most-produced play, both historically and currently. Anyone care to venture a guess? Yes! *A Midsummer Night's Dream*—Lysander to the spurned and slumbering Hermia. Lewis truncates the quote, leaving it dangling a bit awkwardly, rather than nestled into the middle of two rhymed couplets:

> Or as the heresies that men do leave
> Are hated most of those they did deceive;
> So thou, my surfeit and my heresy,
> Of all be hated, but the most of me![3]

I have had the opportunity to work on *A Midsummer Night's Dream* five times in my life, twice as an actor and three times as a director, and I'd like to linger with it for just a few moments. If I were to ask you to briefly describe the actions of the play—just a rudimentary plotline—how successful could you be, in a few sentences? I tried this at home—it's not very easy. It's a play that is a beautifully organic whole, but whose constituent parts seem to have been stitched together from a crazy-quilt dream! In this way it resembles the part of Narnia that offended J. R. R. Tolkien so deeply, a willy-nilly mishmash of species and mythologies, so unlike the systematic world of Middle-earth. *A Midsummer Night's Dream* is a play where characters awake from dreams *eleven times* and immediately turn to the audience to report what they have dreamt about. This is the part of the "influence"

---

[3]William Shakespeare, *A Midsummer Night's Dream*, ed. Harold F. Brooks (London: Routledge, 1994), 50.

conversation that is perhaps most interesting to me, and certainly hardest to quantify—Lewis's surprise visitor, the bounding lion of his dreams.

I am reminded once again of Bergman, sitting in the fundamentalist Lutheran church of his youth:

> While father preached away in the pulpit and the congregation prayed, sang, or listened, I devoted my interest to the church's mysterious world of low arches, thick walls, the smell of eternity, the colored sunlight quivering above the strangest vegetation of medieval paintings and carved figures on ceilings and walls. There was everything that one's imagination could desire—angels, saints, dragons, prophets, devils, humans.[4]

Alan Jacobs reminded me in a recent conversation that for the Elizabethans, the *imagination* was most often cast as something false, something to mistrust. Returning to *A Midsummer Night's Dream,* Duke Theseus of Athens, opining to his new bride on the day of their wedding, would surely have found immediate understanding in his audience for his rationalist's take on the poet's process:

> The poet's eye, in a fine frenzy rolling,
> Doth glance from heaven to earth, from earth to heaven;
> And as imagination bodies forth
> The form of things unknown, the poet's pen
> Turns them to shapes, and gives to airy nothing
> A local habitation and a name.
> Such tricks hath strong imagination,
> That if it would but apprehend some joy,
> It comprehends some bringer of that joy:
> Or, in the night, imagining some fear,
> How easy is a bush supposed a bear![5]

---

[4]Egil Törnqvist, *Between Stage and Screen: Ingmar Bergman Directs* (Amsterdam: Amsterdam University Press, 1995), 95-96.
[5]Shakespeare, *A Midsummer Night's Dream*, 104-5.

I like to imagine that Hippolyta, the vanquished warrior-queen, here allows her hand to rest for the first time on the duke's arm and, in defense of all things "through a mirror, darkly," offers her new husband another view of the imagination:

> But all the stories of the night told over
> And all their minds transfigur'd so together,
> More witnesseth than fancy's images,
> And grows to something of great constancy;
> But howsoever, strange and admirable.[6]

Is Hippolyta saying something about the process we are considering here this evening? I like to think that the young Oxford poet, having no idea yet of what might lie ahead or how his art might grow, is acknowledging something of the possibility of his own teeming imagination being greeted by the imagination of a future reader—and the chance that in that meeting, something completely dependent *on* that meeting ("minds transfigur'd so together," maybe even "something of great constancy") might result. He offers:

> You. Stranger.
> Long before your glance can light upon these words,
> time will have washed away the moment
> when I first took pen to write.
> With all my road before me.
> Yet. Today. If at all. We meet.
> The unfashioned clay ready to both our hands.
> Both hushed to see that which is . . . nowhere
> Yet. Come forth. And be.
> (*Dymer*, Canto I, revised and adapted for emphasis)[7]

[6]Shakespeare, *A Midsummer Night's Dream*, 104-5.
[7]C. S. Lewis, *Dymer*, Canto I.

3

"OUT OF OLD FIELDS THE FLOWERS OF UNBORN SPRINGS"

WHEN LUCY OPENED THE DOOR of the wardrobe she discovered a world inside that would lead to many adventures, not only for herself but for all who have followed her and seen Narnia through her eyes. Lewis opens more than wardrobe doors. Virtually all of his books are thresholds to other worlds of the imagination. What we meet in seed in one book blossoms into full flower or bears rich fruit in another. *Dymer* in many ways is the first of these seed-bearing books; and in this chapter, I am asserting there are features in *Dymer* that hint of things to come from Lewis's pen. Having the advantage and perspective of time, a reader can see:

> the unwearied joy that brings
> Out of old fields the flowers of unborn springs,
> Out of old wars and cities burned with wrong,
> A splendour in the dark, a tale, a song.[1]

I plan to identify some of these themes. Certainly most authors, whose careers span decades, will bring "out of old fields the flowers of unborn springs."

Jody Woerner in her doctoral dissertation notes this about Lewis's fiction: "There does seem to be an unmistakable quality that pervades all his fictional

---

[1] C. S. Lewis, *Dymer: Wade Annotated Edition* in Jerry Root, *Splendour in the Dark: C. S. Lewis's Dymer in His Life and Work* (Downers Grove, IL: IVP Academic 2020), V.29.

works as if he had left behind the scent of some familiar breeze—bright, bracing, and borne from a distant clime."[2] Similarly, author and Lewis scholar David Downing says that there is a "fascinating interconnectedness in all the books; . . . reading any one of them casts light on all the others."[3] Others have observed this as well. For example, J. A. W. Bennett, Lewis's student at Oxford, the man who would take up his chair at Cambridge after Lewis retired, acknowledged this interconnectedness in all his writing. In his inaugural address at Cambridge, Bennett said of Lewis, "The whole man was in all his judgments and activities. . . . His works are all of a piece: a book in one genre will correct, illumine or amplify what is latent in another."[4] Familiarity with Lewis continues to reveal this characteristic of his work. Concepts defined in his non-fiction are illustrated in his imaginative works. A self-effacing comment in one of his literary critical works may merit an entire chapter in one of his religious books. A thought in bud, found in a letter, is manifest in full bloom in an essay. An idea presented by means of an essay becomes the subject of a book. Interconnections reverberate throughout Lewis's work. Such internal amplification suggests that, in many ways, the best interpreter of his work is Lewis. Therefore, it is reasonable to suggest that *Dymer*, Lewis's most significant preconversion book, would also exhibit some degree of interconnectedness with the works that followed.

While there is much here, I am choosing to explore four categories to show where the DNA appears in Lewis's later work. These four areas are first, Dymer's encounter with reality; second, Dymer's encounter with the contemptible; third, Dymer's encounter with his true self as a man weighed and wanting; and lastly, Dymer's quest for meaning. Each category opens a door into things to come.

---

[2]Jody Woerner, "A Dissertation Presented in Partial Fulfillment of the Requirements for the Degree Doctor of Philosophy" (PhD diss., Arizona State University, December 2001), 1.

[3]David C. Downing, *Planets in Peril* (Amherst: University of Massachusetts Press, 1992), 8.

[4]J. A. W. Bennett, "The Humane Medievalist an Inaugural Address," *Critical Essays on C. S. Lewis*, ed. George Watson, (Aldershot, Hauts., England: Scolar Press, 1992), 74. Also in Gilbert, Douglas, and Clyde Kilby, *C. S. Lewis: Images of His World* (Grand Rapids, MI: William B. Eerdmans, 1973), 85.

DYMER ENCOUNTERS REALITY

It is because "reality is iconoclastic" that Dymer bolts from the City. The limitations imposed upon him by the masters of his environment cannot hold up to the complexities of the real world. Furthermore, as Dymer escapes from the City his awareness of the outside world grows constantly larger. It is along these lines each of Dymer's discoveries are made possible, because reality is iconoclastic. This concept, appearing as it first does in Lewis's *Dymer*, will continue to have play throughout the rest of his written work.

Reality is iconoclastic. Dymer, as a character, continually has to modify what he knows and feels. This is as it should be. No matter what we know, more can be known. Truth can always be plumbed deeper and applied more widely to questions we have yet to ask. While it is possible to have a sure word about a matter, we can never have a last word about anything. What we know must be held with an open hand if we hope to grow. Sure words breed confidence in what is known. Yet, the fact that I cannot have a last word requires that confidences be held with humility. I think this is one of the secrets to Lewis's appeal: confidence and humility. For this reason, "reality is iconoclastic" is a theme that reverberates throughout the pages of his published work. The concept first appears in *Dymer*. In the years that followed its publication, Lewis developed the idea in a variety of ways. First, I must review a few examples that appear particularly in Canto I. In stanza 4, we learn that it was the last Platonists who built the city where Dymer was born and lived. They set about their task, "torturing into stone / Each bubble that the Academy had blown." Reality bursts the bubble for Dymer. In stanza 7, we are told:

> For nineteen years they worked upon his soul,
> Refining, chipping, moulding and adorning.
> Then came the moment that undid the whole—
> The ripple of rude life without a warning.

In stanza 8, a breeze from an open window lets in a hint of the outside world. He is distracted from the artificialities of the City and the spectral nature of an indoctrination lecture. Then a brown bird perches on the sill, and Dymer's attention is riveted on the real world outside. He bolts from the City. In stanza 18, having escaped, he now finds himself alone, outside the City walls; the sun has set and he is "hungry and cold." The reality that prompted him, full of promise and expectation, now proves to disappoint. Again, even here, reality is iconoclastic. What is in seed in this narrative poem will continue to bear fruit in all Lewis writes thereafter. What follows below is a mere sampling of the many examples that occur throughout Lewis's books. I do not want what follows to read like a grocery list; nevertheless, I want it to be obvious how big this theme really is and how it effects what he wrote.

Lewis's literary judgments. Before he became a Christian, Lewis writes in *Surprised by Joy*, though he rejected Christianity he was particularly attracted to George Herbert's poetry for his ability to write about what Lewis called "the roughness and density of life."[5] What did he mean by this? Reality is complex and simple descriptions of the world are not satisfying. Lewis was looking for authors who could write about life honestly. He held this value as he wrote *Dymer*. Walter Hooper mentions a paper Lewis read to the Martlets, an Oxford University literary society, stating that "taking art as an expression, it must be the expression of something: and one can't abstract the 'something' from the expression."[6] Hooper says it was "probably a literary milestone for Lewis: he understood how differently others read and judged literature, and he was forced to defend what he loved and believed to be true." Hooper adds, "Lewis was already at work marshalling his ideas and trying them out in the cut-and-thrust debates with his fellow students."[7] Hooper mentions one Martlets meeting

---

[5]C. S. Lewis, *Surprised by Joy* (New York: Harcourt, Brace and Company, 1956), 214.
[6]C. S. Lewis, *Selected Literary Essays*, ed. Walter Hooper (Cambridge: Cambridge University Press, 1969), xii.
[7]Lewis, *Selected Literary Essays*, xii.

where Lewis read a paper on James Stephens. He commented before reading the paper that he knew no biographical details of his subject and was therefore free to focus his remarks on Stephens's work and not be distracted by the details of his life.[8] Lewis, early on, made it his practice to adjust his literary judgments to what actually presented itself on the page of a text. Examples that stretch across the decades can be found in his *Selected Literary Essays*.

The Martlets material mentioned above came from the 1920s and was contemporary to the publication of *Dymer*. The next decade, in 1937, Lewis read a paper on William Morris. He said Morris's stories "express the author's deepest sense of reality, which is subtler and more sensitive than we expect—a mass of 'tensions' as von Hugel would have said."[9] Again, we see the value coming through that "reality is iconoclastic." Later, in 1939, Lewis published *The Personal Heresy: A Controversy*, where he emphasizes that criticism is about texts not authors. The idea, of course, being that the text before you is the reality to which all criticisms must conform; false notions are correctable by appealing to the objectivity of the text itself. Real debate is possible only because the disputants can look to a common, objective source. Again, a seed sown in *Dymer* is still bearing fruit. Furthermore, in Lewis's 1942 essay, "Psycho-Analysis and Literary Criticism," he warns against the Freudian literary critical practice that would project onto a text the assumptions the critic brings to the text. In these cases, people find what they want to find. Nevertheless, reality is iconoclastic; consequently, errors can be set right, but the critic must get beyond the dungeon of self to do it. Also in the forties, Lewis produced the essay "Kipling's World"; here, too, he warns against the tendency toward subjectivism that he sees in Rudyard Kipling's poetry. Lewis calls Kipling the poet of "the Inner Ring," the clique that allows no entry to outsiders, and therefore, no corrections from beyond the limits of what is already known. Kipling is the master of "group think" guarding against any encroachment

---

[8] Lewis, *Selected Literary Essays*, xiii.
[9] Lewis, *Selected Literary Essays*, 224.

from the outside, real world.[10] In the 1950s Lewis still expresses the value that an accurate grasp of reality is necessary for any kind of sound thinking. In his 1954 essay, "A Note on Jane Austen," Lewis shines praise on her work and says she is "the daughter of Dr. Johnson: she inherits his common sense, his morality, even much of his style."[11] Furthermore, Lewis heaps high praise on her work because it exhibits the quality of "undeception." In each of her books, there is a moment when the heroine comes to a realization that she has gotten it all wrong, and not a moment too soon. This is possible because surrender to reality allows the false notion to fracture and the truth to break through.[12] In other words, reality is iconoclastic. In a 1956 essay, "Sir Walter Scott," Lewis sets forth the idea once again, but here he expresses it in unique ways. He draws from what Scott wrote about melancholy, "I think the experience of all bereavements, the daily and hourly setting out of the thoughts upon a familiar road, forgetful of the grim frontier-post that now blocks it, the repeated frustration which renews not only sorrow but the surprise of sorrow, has seldom been more truthfully conveyed."[13] Lewis says of Scott that he was the first of men who taught the feeling for period.[14] That is, that while humans share much in common with all who are *Homo sapiens*, we must take care not to project onto any period values that are peculiar to our own. This is to miss the uniqueness of any age and neglect what a complex thing it is to be human. These things are anticipated in Lewis's *Dymer,* and as has been exhibited, that book is a seedbed for much that springs up throughout the decades in his insightful literary judgments.

Lewis's fiction. This idea embodied in *Dymer* is seen in his fiction as well. All of the heroes in Lewis's fiction are those who constantly make deeper and wider discoveries of the world around them. What they believed and valued at the beginning of a book must give way to accommodation or

[10]Lewis, *Selected Literary Essays*, 232-50.
[11]Lewis, *Selected Literary Essays*, 186.
[12]Lewis, *Selected Literary Essays*, 175-86.
[13]Lewis, *Selected Literary Essays*, 216.
[14]Lewis, *Selected Literary Essays*, 217.

assimilation. Lucy discovers a new world through a wardrobe; Peter, Susan, and Edmund follow. Edmund discovers even the sins of a traitor can be atoned for, and he can still find value and purpose in his life. Eustace discovers a world beyond those depicted in the books he has read, books that never made room for dragons, and fairies, chivalry and courage. Orual, Queen of Glome, must confront those falsehoods within her own heart that have made it impossible to see or accept the reality of the world around her.

In the Space Trilogy, when Ransom first steps foot on Malacandra, Lewis writes, "He gazed about him, and the very intensity of his desire to take in the new world at a glance defeated itself. He saw nothing but colours—colours that refused to form themselves into things. Moreover, he knew nothing yet well enough to see it: you cannot see things until you know roughly what they are."[15] Over time, familiarity with this new world as it strikes his senses allows Ransom to grasp that world and to be enriched by its beauty and complexity. Lewis explains, of Ransom's budding experience of this strange planet, that "Before he learned anything else he learned that Malacandra was beautiful."[16] Lewis experienced something similar to that of Ransom, while just a child. He said he never had an experience of beauty as a boy until his brother brought into the nursery a toy garden on the lid of a biscuit tin. He exclaims in *Surprised by Joy*, "What the real garden had failed to do, the toy garden did. It made me aware of nature."[17] His encounter with one experience of beauty opens the door for him to experience more.

There are some wonderful examples in *Out of the Silent Planet*. Ransom is kidnapped and taken to Mars. He escapes his captors but cannot escape the fact that he is far from earth and the hope of a return seems unlikely. Alone and aware not only of his strange surroundings and potential danger, "He was [also] quite aware of the danger of madness, and applied himself

---

[15]C. S. Lewis, *Out of the Silent Planet* (New York: Macmillian, 1965), 41-42.
[16]Lewis, *Out of the Silent Planet*, 41-42.
[17]Lewis, *Surprised by Joy*, 7.

vigorously to his devotions and his toilet."[18] It is through encounter with the real that Ransom is able to maintain his sanity. Furthermore, among his many adventures, Ransom eventually develops a friendship with a hross named Hyoi, and the two discuss the pleasures of friendship. Hyoi says,

> "A pleasure is full grown only when it is remembered. . . . When you and I met, the meeting was over very shortly, it was nothing. Now it is growing something as we remember it. But still we know so little about it. What will it be when I remember it as I lie down to die, what it makes in me all my days till then—that is the real meeting. The other is only the beginning of it. You say you have poets in your world. Do they not teach you this?"[19]

Again, reality is iconoclastic; all prior notions must give way, and those who surrender to the real enjoy its fruit.

"Reality is iconoclastic," in seed in *Dymer*, is also manifest as Lewis writes over the decades. He writes of these things for children, and should they learn well, perhaps they will maintain something of the childlike wonder of the real world throughout their lives. For example, in *The Lion, the Witch and the Wardrobe*, Peter and Susan are confronted with a conundrum. Their sister Lucy and their brother Edmund are arguing over a point. Lucy claims the two of them went into a strange world called Narnia and they got there through a wardrobe in the Professor's house while playing hide-and-seek. Edmund denies it ever happened. Who speaks the truth, Lucy or Edmund? They ask the Professor about it. The things Lucy says seem very odd, and contrary to anything Peter and Susan have ever experienced. They find it hard to believe her. Yet Edmund typically has been the sibling most prone to fabrication. The Professor says the two older siblings must consider the facts. Lucy is either delusional, or lying, or telling the truth. If there is nothing that suggests she is delusional, and if she has always been a truthful person and Edmund the one generally false,

---

[18]Lewis, *Out of the Silent Planet*, 51.
[19]Lewis, *Out of the Silent Planet*, 73.

then, says the Professor, they should consider that she may likely be speaking the truth. Then the Professor asks, "Why don't they teach logic in these schools, anymore?"[20] Edmund and Susan think they have understood reality and cannot conceive that it could be contrary to their present grasp. They will be surprised. Reality is iconoclastic.

In another example, we find Lucy encountering Aslan for the first time on her second adventure to Narnia. "Aslan," said Lucy, "you're bigger." "That is because you are older, little one," answered he. "Not because you are?" "I am not. But every year you grow, you will find me bigger."[21] Furthermore, Jill, in *The Silver Chair*, knowing nothing about Aslan on this her first visit to Narnia, encounters the lion standing at the only proximate source of water while she is *dying* of thirst. She thinks she knows lions, but she will have to discover there is something unique and different about this lion. In fact, she will never get to the bottom of him. "Reality is iconoclastic"; it begins in *Dymer* and appears in nearly every chapter in all seven of the Narnia books.

Escape beyond the wall. Dymer fled the city and the culture that constrained him. Lewis writes of his escape from the city that he had to go "beyond the wall."[22] Lewis uses a similar motif in his first explicitly Christian book, *The Pilgrim's Regress*. John, the pilgrim, must also escape from Puritania by going beyond a wall. John has looked through a window in the wall surrounding his home. He has seen the vision of an island, and longing awakens in him. He bolts from his home and goes beyond the wall in quest of the island. "Beyond the wall," for John, means more than breaking free from home—it is breaking free of the rigidity that defined his community. The flavor of his escape from Puritania is very similar to what occurs in *Dymer*. John sees something outside of his immediate world and is prompted to pursue it. Yet Lewis, now a Christian author,

[20]C. S. Lewis, *The Lion, the Witch and the Wardrobe* (New York: The Macmillan Company, 1950), 37-40.
[21]C. S. Lewis, *Prince Caspian* (New York: Macmillan Publishing Co., 1951), 117.
[22]Lewis, *Dymer*, I.13.

gives John more direction as he travels. John's quest is a spiritual one. Dymer's pilgrimage is fraught with ambiguity. John, guided by a vision with a path to follow, oscillates between the rigidity of the mountains, representing reason, and the amorphic nature of the swamps that represent the romantic longings of the heart. John finds that Mother Kirk, the church in this allegory, is the one who can unify the quest of mind and heart. The idea of longing is in evidence in both *Dymer* and *Regress*, but the Lewis of *Regress* is clearer about where the longing will lead. Nevertheless, something of escape appears in *Dymer* and is seen in Lewis's later work. For John, staying on the path is a process of constant correction—also an example of "reality is iconoclastic."

Escape to nature. There are events in *Dymer* where he wearies of situations that have caused him deep sadness and concern. Each time, he is revived by nature and something numinous that seems to transcend her. It is the real that renews him; it is reality that revives. Wandering through woods and over a mountain, Dymer comes to a place where he sleeps. His dream is tranquil. In it, he hears a lark that

> Sang out of heaven, "The world will never end,"
> Sang from the gates of heaven, "Will never end."
> Sang till it seemed there was no other thing
> But bright space and one voice set there to sing.[23]

In this dream, Dymer is wooed by the singing lark to look at something so large and compelling it eclipses all other things from his view. It is set apart and distinct from the ever-changing and mutable world in which he has found himself by virtue of its immutability and "never-ending" qualities. Lewis begins the next two stanzas with the words "It seemed," and here he sets out to interpret the song of the lark for his readers, thus making his aims very clear. The lark sang, "I AM"; and Lewis says from this I AM "flows the justice that men call Divine."[24] George Sayer observes, "He is

---

[23]Lewis, *Dymer*, V.27.
[24]Lewis, *Dymer*, V.28.

rescued by contact with complete and integrated, God-made creatures, whom he can accept as they really are."[25] But, as he awakes, Dymer believes that what he heard was only a mere bird piping, and is unwilling to attribute this to any kind of transcendence. The canto ends as Dymer takes to his pilgrim road once again.

DYMER AND THE CONTEMPTIBLE

Dymer experiences three categories of the contemptible, that is, various forms of evil. Each of these categories will show up later in Lewis's books. First, there are the conditioners who created the City where he lives; second is Bran the anarchist; and lastly, the subjectivist magician.

The conditioners. Dymer was born and raised in the City designed by social engineers and conditioners. He knows nothing else but this one experience of a very small region of the world. One would think he would be content with the one thing he knows since his limited experience gives him nothing with which to compare or judge the world around him. Nevertheless, his heart grows immediately discontent on the day he notices a real spring day. Spring is real; by contrast, the world of the City is spectral. The artificiality of the City cannot compare with even a moment of the real.

Contempt of the utopian state is one particular value exhibited in *Dymer*. Of the City of Dymer's birth, Lewis writes:

> No hour was left unchartered in that town,
> And love was in a schedule and the State
> Chose for eugenic reasons who should mate
> With whom, and when.[26]

Skepticism concerning the omnicompetent state preexists Lewis's conversion to Christianity, as is evident in *Dymer*. This skepticism is presented in at least three other works by Lewis: his critique of "the conditioners" in

---

[25]George Sayer, "C. S. Lewis's *Dymer*," *Seven: An Anglo-American Literary Review* 1 (March 1980), 106.

[26]Lewis, *Dymer*, I.3. See also Canto I, stanzas 4, 6, and 7.

The Abolition of Man[27]; his exposé of the N.I.C.E. (the National Institute for Coordinated Experiments) in *That Hideous Strength*[28]; and the bureaucracy of hell satirized in *The Screwtape Letters*. Impatience with such things also undergirds the offhand comments made about "Experiment House" in *The Silver Chair*.[29] Two of these embodiments are worth noting with some detail.

The most developed exposition of concern about "conditioners" is found in chapter three of *The Abolition of Man*. Here Lewis is deconstructing a sixth form grammar book called *The Control of Language* by Alec King and Martin Ketley. Not wishing to embarrass the authors, Lewis calls them Gaius and Titius, and refers to the text as *The Green Book*. Lewis points out that the authors, attempting to teach grammar, have inadvertently smuggled all kinds of philosophical assumptions into the minds of their readers. They begin by telling a story of Samuel Taylor Coleridge at a waterfall on the river Clyde.[30] There are two tourists present; one calls the waterfall "pretty," the other calls it "sublime." Coleridge endorses the second description and is dismissive of the first. The authors of *The Green Book* declare that Coleridge had no right to make such a judgment for neither of the tourists was making a statement about the waterfall, but merely a statement about their own feelings concerning the waterfall. Lewis expresses deep concern at this point. First, because all true statements are validated only when there is a reality that supports the truth claim. The tourists were not making comments about their feelings but about the waterfall. Both had something positive to say, but Coleridge endorsed the second because it was more robustly descriptive. Furthermore, Lewis takes issue with Gaius and Titius, because he believes statements of emotion can be in harmony with reason. We can talk about

[27]Lewis, *The Abolition of Man*, 38ff.
[28]C. S. Lewis, *That Hideous Strength: A Modern Fairy-Tale for Grown-Ups*. (London: John Lane, The Bodley Head, 1949), 21.
[29]C. S. Lewis, *The Silver Chair* (New York: Macmillan, 1953), 5.
[30]Lewis, *Abolition of Man*, 7. Dorothy Wordsworth records this incident in her *Grasmere Journals 1803* and identifies the waterfall as the Cora Linn Waterfall on the river Clyde.

just sentiments whenever emotions are supported by a context in which those feelings are merited. Happiness at a birthday party is proper to that occasion, but giddiness at a funeral is inappropriate (unless we owed a lot of money to the person who passed away). Lewis calls these appropriate responses "objective value." He uses the word *Tao* as a shorthand for this appropriateness. Furthermore, he questions how it is that Gaius and Titius can make judgments that Coleridge had no right to be discriminating of the comments by the tourists. If Coleridge had no right to judge, then neither do the authors of *The Green Book*, but judge they do. While Lewis suggests reasons these authors might employ to validate their judgment, each is less than objective and leads to a kind of self-referentialism. As Lewis writes *The Abolition of Man*, he sees this kind of self-reference as dangerous to the society that accepts it. When such subjectivism is in ascendancy, and a party is no longer tethered to that form of objective value that overarches rulers and ruled alike, that party will likely become utilitarian and tyrannical. The views of *The Abolition of Man* are in evidence in this first category of evil as depicted in *Dymer*. In *The Abolition of Man*, he calls those who ascend to power in the omnicompetent state "the Conditioners;" the framers of this City are their progenitors.

These architects of the City in *Dymer* are also suggestive of characters to be met in Lewis's third Space novel, *That Hideous Strength*. In that novel the reader encounters a nefarious organization ironically named N.I.C.E. These people are anything but nice. They begin by conducting experiments on animals and drift toward doing experiments on human beings. They have turned their backs on objective value and justify their evil acts as beneficial to the human race; they produce a horror. Again, seeds for such depictions have their origin in *Dymer*.

The anarchist. In Canto IV, Dymer discovers the contemptible in another kind of character: the anarchist. In his wandering Dymer stumbles upon a mortally wounded man who has been blinded and whose hands are severed. Dymer assumes the role of father confessor to this man and hears his story. He learns that in the wake of his flight from the City an anarchist named Bran has stirred up a rebellion and thrown the City into chaos. To his horror, Dymer learns that Bran used his name as a banner to incite anarchy. Those that follow Bran rationalize and justify the evil of their acts. The wounded man says,

> Once the lying spirit of a cause
> With maddening words dethrones the mind of men,
> They're past the reach of prayer. The eternal laws
> Hate them. Their eyes will not come clean again,
> But doom and strong delusion drive them.[31]

The anarchist, having stepped away from traditional morality, has no standard by which to judge his acts, or anyone else's for that matter. He has no objective value validating others who follow him. He spins his sense of right or wrong out from himself as a spider spins its web to ensnare the unsuspecting. Certainly, something of this characteristic is depicted in the anarchist Lewis meets in *The Great Divorce*.[32] Furthermore, Lewis writes explicitly about the tendency that justifies evil. His familiarity with Aristotle's concept of *akrasia* (to lose command of one's moral clarity through rationalization) is footnoted in *The Abolition of Man*. Lewis draws from the *Nicomachean Ethics*.[33] Also, in *A Preface to Paradise Lost*, he acknowledges, "Continued disobedience makes conscience blind."[34] These rationalizing anarchists are further depicted in the dwarves of *The Pilgrim's Regress* who, in that allegory, represent the brown shirts and black shirts of the Italian and Nazi Fascist parties.

The subjectivist. Lewis has many memorable villains in his fiction. The magician in *Dymer* is, in some ways, a prototype of all of them. Nevertheless, as a subjectivist, he is a precursor to the ghosts in *The Great Divorce*, and to Weston in *Out of the Silent Planet* and *Perelandra*. Weston is by far Lewis's most fully developed evil character rivaling the White Witch of

---

[31]Lewis, *Dymer*, IV.29.

[32]C. S. Lewis, *The Great Divorce* (New York: Macmillan, 1950), 6-14.

[33]Lewis. *The Abolition of Man*, 31. Here Lewis cites *Ethics* sections 1095b, 1140b, and 1151a.

[34]C. S. Lewis, *A Preface to Paradise Lost* (London: Oxford University Press, 1942), 10.

Narnia. In fact, Weston is so evil he loses his humanity and is referred to simply as the "Unman" in *Perelandra*. His DNA can be found in the magician of *Dymer*, for both lose their humanity while denying the inexorable claims of objective value. Of such as these, Lewis will later write in *The Abolition of Man*, "Stepping outside the *Tao*, they have stepped into the void."[35] The magician is not satisfied with his own contemptible life, but must ensnare others as well. Dymer is drawn into the magician's house. All reference to the reality of the outside world is shut out. Dymer is coerced into delusional dreams; he is caught in the magician's web.

The magician coaxes Dymer into the world of the unreal by means of spells and magic, a motif similar to the one Lewis will employ nearly thirty years later in *The Silver Chair*. There a Green Witch ensnares Prince Rilian of Narnia, Eustace Scrubb, Jill Pole, and Puddleglum the Marshwiggle into a world of her making in order to control them by casting a spell on them. By remembering the real over against the witch's artificial world, as painful as that would prove to be for Puddleglum, the company is able, at last, to break the enchantment.[36] Similarly, this charlatan, the magician of *Dymer*, is thwarted by reality. A real thirst for real water causes Dymer to awaken from the false dreams. He discovers that the magician has killed the lark. And true to form with all of Lewis's evil characters, he is not only cruel to animals; the Magician turns on Dymer and shoots him. These passages in *Dymer* will have play in Lewis's later work. These same evil characters continue to surface.

DYMER WEIGHED AND WANTING

As a character, Dymer's shortcomings are often measured against his circumstances. He is a flawed man. Unaware of his own shortcomings, he will be weighed on the scales and found wanting. Just before he bolts from the

---

[35]Lewis, *The Abolition of Man*, 77.

[36]Lewis, *The Silver Chair*, chapter 12, "The Queen of Underland." It is there that Lewis reminds his readers how the real world, even with its pains, can restore one from the falsehoods of the subjectivists. He writes, "There is nothing like a good shock of pain for dissolving certain kinds of magic," 154.

City, Lewis writes, "That moment saw the soul of Dymer hang / In the balance."[37] Lewis is alluding to a biblical image, the account of Belshazzar, the Babylonian king at the handwriting on the wall in the book of Daniel. One of the items scribbled on the wall Daniel interprets as "You have been weighed in the balances and found wanting" (Dan 5:27). The preconverted Lewis was an honest literary scholar. He knew his Bible and thus benefitted from its images when he saw them and used them when it fit his purposes. In the balances, self-awareness will come to Dymer as his adventures unfold. Furthermore, his processes of self-discovery are not unlike what Lewis will depict in his later works.

The mirrored image and painful self-awareness. Dymer bolts from the city ignorant of the consequences of his act. He seems to sense no guilt for striking his instructor and murdering him. He is utterly unaware of the rebellion that will arise in his wake. In one sense, he is free, but as his story unfolds, it will remain to be seen if he will emerge an anarchist like Bran or gain wisdom through his errors and trials. If anything, his newfound freedom seems to have given him an abundance of temporary self-confidence. In Canto II, he comes upon a manor house. The door is open wide and he feels free to enter. There was light from every direction and no shadows were cast. His eyes are darting in every direction, "The oppression of huge places wrapped him round."[38] Suddenly he turns a corner and sees "far off, a wild-eyed, naked man . . . That came to meet him." Dymer, to defend himself, lunges at his attacker only to find he was looking into a mirror and was afraid of his own image. Throughout the time he is in the manor house Dymer is being "undeceived,"[39] he is entering a place of self-discovery; reality is iconoclastic. Lewis writes, "The boy went on . . . manly playing / At manhood."[40] It is in this manor house that Dymer has his tryst with the woman. Leaving the manor the next day, he realizes how he has

---

[37]Lewis, *Dymer*, I.9.
[38]Lewis, *Dymer*, II.4.
[39]Lewis, *Dymer*, II.10.
[40]Lewis, Dymer, II.12.

used her. He feels guilt for the first time. Seeking to reenter the house and set right his wrongs, he is rebuffed by an old hag. She defeats him blow after blow, and Dymer again and again must realize that he has far less courage and significantly less strength than he imagined. The manor is a place of self-discovery, and this self-discovery begins with the incident at the mirror. The use of a mirror to enable characters to see themselves as they truly are, as first used here in *Dymer*, is a motif often found in Lewis.

In *The Great Divorce*, Lewis finds himself as a character in hell. He sees a queue and joins the line waiting for who knows what? A bus arrives and Lewis boards the bus. The characters on board are despicable people. Fights constantly break out and Lewis finds himself in the jumble sitting next to someone new every so often. In each case, the character begins to tell his story and Lewis is shocked at the despicable nature of each of the passengers. The narrative suggests to the reader that the Lewis in the book thinks of himself better than he thinks of these deplorable people. Then, just as the bus arrives at the threshold of heaven, light pours into the bus and Lewis looks down the aisle. He sees up front, by the driver, that there is a mirror; and he sees reflected in it his own image.[41] Lewis's character, like Dymer, is undeceived.

The Voyage of the Dawn Treader is a story that begins, "There was a boy called Eustace Clarence Scrubb, and he almost deserved it."[42] This comes from the pen of Clive Staples Lewis, who was sure nobody deserved to be named Clive Staples. While Lewis seems to feel for Eustace, Eustace himself raises no cause for empathy. He may be a boy, but beneath the skin of a boy beats the heart of a dragon. He is with his cousins Edmund and Lucy when he is magically drawn into Narnia through a painting. The three children find themselves on the deck of a Narnian sailing ship, joining King Caspian and his crew. Caspian is on a quest to find the seven lost lords of Narnia, and also to take the chivalrous mouse Reepicheep to Aslan's country in order to fulfill a prophecy that was uttered over him at his birth. In the magic of that world, Eustace turns outwardly into the very dragon he has

---

[41]Lewis, *The Great Divorce*, 16.
[42]C. S. Lewis, *The Voyage of the Dawn Treader* (New York: Collier Books, 1971), 1.

always been in his heart. He discovers the reality while gazing into a pond.[43] The water, like a mirror, reflects back to him his dragonesque state. He sees himself, truly, for the first time and grieves. It is an important step toward his transformation. Here the image of the mirror, first used by Lewis in *Dymer*, is also used in *The Voyage of the Dawn Treader*.

In Lewis's novel *Till We Have Faces*, the motif is used again. Orual, Queen of Glome, is writing of her complaint against the gods. The goddess Ungit embodies all that she hates. Her anger and hostility is virtually unquenched. Unfortunately, she is blind to every flaw in her own character. Nevertheless, transforming moments occur for her as she marks the process from horrifying self-awareness to transformation while peering at her image reflected in a mirror throughout the novel.[44] Lewis uses these images to show that real change begins only if we can see ourselves as others see us. The mirror used in *Dymer* grows in significance each time Lewis employs it.

Dymer's self-awareness is only beginning; he must discover more about himself. Having been rebuffed by the hag, he demands of her access to see the woman from the night before. In his demand, he shouts out, "She is mine!"[45] The reader readily sees what Dymer has yet to know. Anyone reading Lewis's *The Great Divorce* has seen this Dymeresque sentiment in the ghosts of the controlling mother[46] and the controlling wife;[47] and in the controlling self-interest of Mrs. Fidget, who is the embodiment of the abuses of *storge* in *The Four Loves*;[48] and of the vicar in "The Sermon and the Lunch."[49] Furthermore, this kind of possessiveness cannot escape notice in Queen Orual's attempts to control those she says she loves: Psyche, the Fox, and Bardia. She confuses love with rationalized self-interest and what prevails is the controlling expectation that things have to be as she

---

[43]Lewis, *The Voyage of the Dawn Treader*, 75.

[44]C. S. Lewis, *Till We Have Faces: A Myth Retold* (San Diego: Harcourt Brace & Company, 1984).

[45]Lewis, *Dymer*, III.20.

[46]Lewis, *The Great Divorce*, 90-96.

[47]Lewis, *The Great Divorce*, 83-89.

[48]Lewis, *The Four Loves*, 60-62.

[49]C. S. Lewis, *God in the Dock: Essays on Theology and* Ethics, ed. Walter Hooper (Grand Rapids, MI: William B. Eerdmans, 1970), 282-86.

must have them be. In fact, Psyche says to her, "You are indeed teaching me about kinds of love I did not know. . . . I am not sure whether I like your kind better than hatred."[50] This possessiveness and control are also in evidence in Jadis, Queen of Charn, who speaks the "deplorable word" to save herself while destroying all the people of Charn. She becomes the White Witch of Narnia who makes it always winter and never Christmas. These things first appear in *Dymer* and proliferate throughout the Lewis books that follow.

Souls in the balances. Lewis writes that Dymer's soul is in the balance. This image also appears in "The Weight of Glory." Lewis contends that there are no ordinary people. Everyone we meet is a soul in the balances moving towards everlasting horrors or everlasting glories. Lewis reminds us that we bear the burden of our neighbor's glory, for our treatment of others nurtures them, hopefully, to Joy, but our ill treatment of others may equally awaken bitterness and jealousy that corrodes and destroys.

As Dymer journeys we are told, "Out of the unscythed grass the nettle grew."[51] It is a telling comment; it seems to allude not only to the nettles in nature, but perhaps also to the nettles and weeds still growing in Dymer's soul. Dymer is quick to assume that the evil in his world must be attributed to the gods. What occurs here is a prequel to much Lewis has to say in later works about the problem of evil and suffering. Here, too, it is easy to slough off suffering and attribute it all to God's poor management of his world. But Dymer is given complaint mixed with doubt. As a man in the balance, he wonders,

> A man must crouch to face
> Infinite malice, watching at all hours,
> Shut Nature out—give her no moment's space
> For entry. The first needs of our race
> Are walls, a den, a cover. Traitor I
> Who first ran out beneath the open sky.[52]

---

[50]Lewis, *Till We Have Faces*, 165.
[51]Lewis, *Dymer*, III.8.
[52]Lewis, *Dymer*, V.14.

Here he is angry with the gods. He would blame the gods. He fears the gods. He would hide from them. Nevertheless, as a man in the balance, humility emerges as he begins to second-guess his bolt from the City and to realize the pain it triggered. Dymer reflects,

> "Our fortress and fenced place I made to fall,
> I slipt the sentries and let in the foe.
> I have lost my brothers and my love and all.
> Nothing is left but me. Now let me go.
> I have seen the world stripped naked and I know.
> Great God, take back your world. I will have none
> Of all your glittering gauds but death alone."[53]

He is caught in the balances and would make sense of himself and his world, with all of its pain and sorrows. So, too, this theme in *Dymer* reverberates in Lewis.

DYMER AND THE QUEST FOR MEANING

As the story develops, Dymer, more and more, seeks to make sense of his experience. From the beginning of the poem, as he bolts from the City and rushes out into the outer world, he shouts, "Trembling darkness, trembling green, / What do you mean, wild wood, what do you mean?" The narrator explains, "Perhaps he half believed / Some answer yet would come to his desire."[54] Dymer hears distant music and it brings tears to his eyes: "[It] turn[ed] the young man's feet to pilgrimage."[55] Celebrating his liberty, he shouts, "I am the wanderer, new born, newly freed,"[56] and adds, "As I fled I wondered / Into whose alien story I had blundered."[57]

Sehnsucht *and the pilgrim's quest.* The moment Dymer longs to make sense of his experience, Lewis links the quest for meaning with the awakening

---

[53]Lewis, *Dymer*, V.15.
[54]Lewis, *Dymer*, I.20.
[55]Lewis, *Dymer*, I.24.
[56]Lewis, *Dymer*, II.20.
[57]Lewis, *Dymer*, I.22.

of desire. At this time in Lewis's own life, the object of his desire was unclear. Nevertheless, he links desire and the quest to find its object here in *Dymer*. Could this be an indication of where Lewis was at this moment in his own pilgrimage and how he was beginning to connect the dots? If so, it reveals yet another reason why *Dymer* is an interesting and significant literary artifact in Lewis studies. Clearly soulful longing and the quest for meaning are often linked in Lewis, and apart from a few brief mentions in *Spirits in Bondage*, what will become a common theme throughout Lewis's work is represented in *Dymer* in its infancy. In Lewis's later work he calls this longing "joy." In fact, his autobiography, *Surprised by Joy*, focuses primarily on this topic: the awakening of desire and the quest to find its proper object. Lewis uses a host of synonyms for the longing: "sweet desire," "the inconsolable secret," "*Sehnsucht*," and "nostalgia." It is this longing coupled with the quest for meaning that prompts Dymer's pilgrimage.

This longing that prompts one to quest, while first seen here in *Dymer*, reverberates throughout Lewis. It is evident in Ransom in the Space Trilogy. All the major characters in the Narnia books are moved by it. As has been mentioned, it is at the very center of John's quest in *The Pilgrim's Regress*. Lewis alludes to such desire in his sermons, particularly "*De Futilitate*,"[58] "Learning in War-Time,"[59] and "The Weight of Glory."[60] All of his popular apologetic works cultivate the theme of longing. Furthermore, Lewis uses this as an "argument from desire." It is something God puts in the hearts of those he seeks to woo to himself. The awakening to longing that Lewis experienced as a child when his older brother Warren brought a toy garden into the nursery occurred long before he wrote *Dymer*, so we know this desire and its accompanying quest were alive in him when he wrote this poem.[61] We recognize in seed here what would fill the pages of the works that followed.

[58]C. S. Lewis, *Christian Reflections*, ed. Walter Hooper (Grand Rapids, MI: William B. Eerdmans, 1967), 57-71.
[59]C. S. Lewis, "On Learning in War-Time" *The Weight of Glory*. New York: Macmillan. 1949.
[60]Lewis, "On Learning in War-Time."
[61]Lewis, *Surprised by Joy*, 7.

Further sense-making: an encounter with a goddess. After the magician wounds Dymer, he meets up with a goddess. In fact, he discovers that she was, in an embodied state, the woman of his tryst in the manor. In Canto III, after his frustrated attempt to reenter the castle, he cries out against the gods and demands that they answer him, but there is no answer.[62] Those who know Lewis's *Till We Have Faces* cannot fail to see the resemblance between Queen Orual's angry cry and Dymer's. Orual has kept a journal of her complaints against the gods. At the end of her life, she comes to a resolution. "I ended my first book with the words *no answer*. I know now, Lord, why you utter no answer. You are yourself the answer. Before your face questions die away. What other answer would suffice?"[63] Something of this is also seen in the account of the Episcopal Ghost in *The Great Divorce*. The Ghost is told by a glorified friend, "I will bring you to the land not of questions but of answers, and you shall see the face of God."[64]

Unlike Orual, who cannot not see the things of God, Dymer receives a visit from this goddess. He complains that she has come too late, and registers his dissatisfaction. A dialogue follows as Dymer complains about his encounter at the manor,

> "You came in human shape, in sweet disguise
> Wooing me, lurking for me in my path,
> Hid your eternal cold with woman's eyes,
> Snared me with shows of love—and all was lies."
> She answered, "For our kind must come to all
> If bidden, but in the shape for which they call."[65]

Here are ideas Lewis develops later, though what he comes to write will be informed by faith. In *Surprised by Joy*, he suggests that Hamlet could only meet Shakespeare if Shakespeare wrote himself into the play. What he

---

[62]Lewis, *Dymer*, III.31-32.

[63]Lewis, *Till We Have Faces*, 308.

[64]Lewis, *The Great Divorce*, 36.

[65]Lewis, *Dymer*, VIII.13. Note also the two stanzas that follow, VIII.14-15, for more on this theme.

writes about the incarnation in *Mere Christianity* and in his essay "The Grand Miracle" is, to some degree, prefigured here.

As the dialogue with the goddess unfolds, Dymer complains further that he has suffered and that the gods would know nothing of this. She immediately corrects him with these words:

> "The gods themselves know pain, the eternal forms.
> In realms beyond the reach of cloud, and skies
> Nearest the ends of air, where comes no storms
> Nor sound of earth, I have looked into their eyes
> Peaceful and filled with pain beyond surmise,
> Filled with an ancient woe man cannot reach
> One moment though in fire; yet calm their speech."[66]

The words reveal a sensitivity on behalf of the goddess one would not have expected from Lewis at this time in his life.

In this visitation, we see hints of what Lewis eventually writes in *The Problem of Pain*, "God saw the crucifixion in the act of creating the first nebula."[67] What would Lewis have the goddess mean in *Dymer*, when she says the gods are familiar with human suffering? Lewis may be suggesting that the gods know a sort of Platonic ideal of pain and that is all. On the other hand, the Lewis of *The Problem of Pain* writes that, because of the incarnation, there is more than merely the idea, there is the existential reality—God the Son entered into the world of human brokenness, sin, and suffering. Nevertheless, what is in *Dymer* opens the door on a grand theme that reverberates through much of what is to follow in Lewis. So much of what he will write either hints at or explicitly investigates matters of theodicy. What is clear from *Dymer* is that Lewis had a sophisticated grasp of Christian theodicy. He knew much before his conversion. The problem was not with lack of knowledge but lack of belief.

---

[66]Lewis, *Dymer*, VIII.9-11.
[67]Lewis, *The Problem of Pain*, 72.

Lewis wrote to Arthur Greeves and said explicitly, "I'm not Dymer"; nevertheless, it may be through *Dymer* that those interested have a window into the transformation going on in Lewis.[68]

> Why do they [the gods] lure to them such spirits as mine,
> The weak, the passionate, and the fool of dreams?
> When better men go safe and never pine
> With whisperings at the heart, soul-sickening gleams
> Of infinite desire, and joy that seems
> The promise of full power? For it was they,
> The gods themselves, that led me on this way.[69]

Dymer felt it was the gods that provoked him to flee the City. He complains they goaded him by desire. He demands an answer.

> "Give me the truth! I ask not now for pity.
> When gods call, can the following them be sin?
> Was it false light that lured me from the City?
> Where was the path—without it or within?
> Must it be one blind throw to lose or win?
> Has heaven no voice to help? Must things of dust
> Guess their own way in the dark?" She said, "They must."[70]

Suddenly Dymer turns to ask another question; the goddess is gone.

It is just after his encounter with the goddess that Dymer begins to make sense of his circumstances and discover his identity. The reality of an encounter with the goddess has been truly iconoclastic. He recounts the many Dymers he has been. The Dymer of the City, the Dymer that knew not Bran, the Dymer of the forest glade, the Dymer of his many adventures. Each he says he has sloughed off; and there is one more, yet to die.[71] The

---

[68]Lewis, *The Collected Letters*, ed. Walter Hooper, vol. 1, Family Letters 1905-1931 (London: Harper Collins, 2000), 644.
[69]Lewis, *Dymer*, VIII.11.
[70]Lewis, *Dymer*, VIII.12.
[71]Lewis, *Dymer*, VIII.22-24.

quest for meaning and understanding will always require adjustment of thought and life. Dymer does not fully see his way clear, but Lewis would come to understand this sure enough. When Joy Davidman, during the Christmas season of 1952, visited Lewis at the Kilns, she asked him to sign her copy of *The Great Divorce*. Remember what he wrote: "There are three images in my mind which I must continually forsake and replace with better ones: the false image of God, the false image of my neighbours, and the false image of myself."[72]

CONCLUSION

We have only looked at a sampling of the big ideas in *Dymer*. Because so much found in the later Lewis can trace its origins to this book, it must be seen as a significant literary artifact for serious Lewis scholarship. I would like to summarize the big ideas.

Dymer's encounter with reality emphasizes the biggest concept in all of Lewis's books: reality is iconoclastic. The idea has its first major exposition in *Dymer*. Furthermore, this approach to reality and its power to shape understanding as well as correct misunderstanding was at the heart of his objectivist commitments, and influenced him all his life. It drove him from the falsities of his childhood faith; it drove him back to Christianity when his atheism and materialism could not measure up to intense scrutiny. It was the concept that allowed him to go deeper in the faith once he was convinced of its objectivity and truth. He wrote, "If our religion is something objective, then we must never avert our eyes from those elements in it which seem puzzling or repellant; for it will be precisely the puzzling or the repellant which conceals what we do not yet know and need to know."[73] Consequently, he was able to illumine the way for others convincingly, because he continually honed and refined his faith. There is little or no question-begging and equivocation in his writing. In *Dymer* we catch this early in Lewis.

---

[72]Walter Hooper, *C. S. Lewis: A Companion Guide* (San Francisco: Harper Collins, 1996), 61.
[73]Lewis, "The Weight of Glory," *Transposition*, 26.

Dymer's encounter with things contemptible gives rise to the evil characters that make their way in his other books: Conditioners, anarchists, the self-referential and utilitarian. Lewis saw these characteristics of evil years before his own conversion, and they gave him pause. He knew that subjectivism detaches itself from reality and leads to evil, thereby diminishing one's humanity. This also is seen early in *Dymer*.

Dymer's encounter with his true self as a man weighed and wanting reflects another early theme. Everyone is caught in the balances. Honesty and humility are the prerequisites to see that this is so. This recognition by Lewis eventually develops into a sense of urgency, particularly in his apologetic works. Almost as a prophet crying in the wilderness he will write, "Now, today, this moment, is our chance to choose the right side."[74] Perhaps this urgency has authority, and authenticity, because of Lewis's own long pilgrimage and what he learned along the way. We find the themes in *Dymer* near the beginning of that process in Lewis.

Dymer also exhibits the quest for meaning. He tries to make sense of his experience and is driven by three things: "reality is iconoclastic"; the longings of the heart; and a growing awareness of the numinous. These have long play in Lewis's life. They constantly show up in his apologetic work. He appeals to them in his desire to assist others in their own pilgrimages to faith. Here again, *Dymer* is a fountainhead for these themes.

Each of the above categories opens a door into things to come. I actually enjoy *Dymer*. I like reading it over and over again. And, I hope, for years to come, that it will be read and referenced as an important literary artifact in Lewis studies, a splendour in the dark.

[74]Lewis, *Mere Christianity*, 52.

RESPONSE

Miho Nonaka

LIKE THE LAST TWO RESPONDENTS to Dr. Jerry Root's Hansen lectures, Dr. Jeffry Davis and Professor Mark Lewis, I am no specialist of C. S. Lewis, and it is with some apprehension that I share my own thoughts inspired by the final installment of Dr. Root's paper on Lewis's epic poem. "My only hope, it seems, is to find my lane and stay in it," said Professor Mark Lewis, in the beginning of his response. It was a great framing device. He was going to offer his perspective, not as a Lewis scholar or a literary critic, but as an actor and a theater maker. In order not to crumple under the pressure of the task at hand, I am convinced that I should follow Professor Lewis's lead "to find my lane and stay in it." This, of course, means that I must first tackle the question, What and where in the world is my lane?

Let me start with an anecdote. Earlier this year, I was talking to my family about Dr. Root's lecture series. My mother-in-law, a well-respected psychologist, asked me to explain what happens in *Dymer*. I did my best to summarize the poem for her: the protagonist's exit from the utopian republic; his dreamy union with "the breathing body of a girl"[1] (the fact that he doesn't know her name or what her face looks like doesn't deter him from claiming "she is mine"[2]); his meeting with a magician who urges him to "Dream again / And deeper"[3] in order to find the girl once more; and his eventual death at the hands of a monster who turns out to be his

---

[1] C. S. Lewis, *Dymer*, II.32.
[2] Lewis, *Dymer*, III.20.
[3] Lewis, *Dymer*, VI.24.

progeny as a result of the aforementioned intercourse with the girl whose name he still doesn't know. Before I could finish, my mother-in-law interrupted me by saying, "You know poets use drugs, don't you?" She continued, "It's either they were on cocaine or they should've been on cocaine, so that they could write better stuff." While I was speechless, what I really wanted to say to her was: *but your daughter-in-law is a poet too!*

Though not by any logic, this anecdote emboldens me to establish that part of my lane is being a poet, with or without cocaine. Another part of the lane has to do with where I was born and grew up. My first encounter with C. S. Lewis was through a Japanese translation. I was ten years old when I first laid my hand on a hardcover copy of one of the famed Narnia books from the school library. It was *The Lion, the Witch and the Wardrobe*, which was translated as 『ライオンと魔女』, "The Lion and the Witch," skipping "the Wardrobe" because, that way, the title falls exactly in seven syllables (*ra・i・o・n・to・ma・jo*). I am from the country of haiku, after all.

One of the most tantalizing things about foreign literature to a child, however awkward the translation may sound to her ear, is the description of food. In my mind, what distinguishes each book in the Little House on the Prairie series is not so much the plot as the host of exotic foods Laura and Almanzo are consuming—from hickory-smoked venison to molasses-on-snow candy, vanity cake, sourdough bread, eggnog, and spicy apple pie. With *Mary Poppins*, I paid far more attention to the rhubarb she buys for pie making, rather than her smug narcissism or morally dubious attitude toward the Banks children she nannies. From another of Lewis's Narnia books, *The Magician's Nephew*, I still remember Digory's description of Narnia: "It was a rich place: as rich as plum cake."[4] It made a visceral impression on me. Narnia was a realm of foreign sweetness, density, and pungency, like "the land of spices" in George Herbert's poem, "Prayer (I)." It is as though food becomes the source of what Lewis called "*Sehnsucht*," the sweet, inconsolable longing for those readers who have

---

[4]C. S. Lewis, *The Magician's Nephew* (New York: Macmillan Publishing Company, 1970), 29.

access to literary work only through translation—because they have no way of knowing or tasting the original.

As you might have guessed by now, in *The Lion and the Witch*, what piqued my curiosity first was the Turkish delight the Witch offers to Edmund, except that it was translated as something entirely different. This is understandable, given that there are no comparable sweets in Japan. Moreover, if the translator were to give a word-by-word translation, the name would have sounded dangerously close to pornography. The translation was published in 1966, and in Japan between the 1950s and the mid-1980s, the term "Turkish bath" meant a type of brothel/massage parlor. (The term was changed to "soap land" after a Turkish exchange student from Tokyo University made an effective public protest, God bless him.)

This is to say, in the Japanese translation, Turkish delight became "プリン," a kind of custard pudding or flan, which is a common dessert in Japan. Imagine reading the following passage:

> The Queen let another drop fall from her bottle onto the snow, and instantly there appeared a round box, tied with green silk ribbon, which, when opened, turned out to contain several pounds of the best [custard pudding]. Each piece was sweet and light to the very center and Edmund had never tasted anything more delicious.[5]

I was puzzled. In Japan, custard pudding/flan was sold in individual plastic cups, never in a box. Since no cups were mentioned, I didn't understand how each jiggly flan could maintain its shape among all the other flans in a box. And why does the author make a point of adding that it was "sweet and light to the very center" (in Japanese, it read "fluffy and sweet"[6]), when the consistency of custard should be the same throughout unless some unfortunate curdling occurred?

---

[5]C. S. Lewis, *The Lion, the Witch and the Wardrobe* (New York: Macmillan Publishing Company, 1970), 32.
[6]C. S. Lewis, *Raion to majo*, trans. Teiji Seta (Tokyo: Iwanami Shoten, 1985), 54.

I didn't dwell on it too long, though. Since I was a child, I have never been a consistent logical thinker, and I blithely accepted the physics-defying nature of these descriptions. Perhaps it was the Witch's magic that kept a bunch of flans from slipping and bumping against each other. When the Witch says, "It is a lovely place, my house. . . . There are whole rooms full of [flans],"[7] I simply pictured a huge fridge-like castle with a multitude of self-contained flans like eggy pyramids levitating in the air. It was surely a magical sight.

After that, my attention shifted to the delightful fish dinner at the Beavers', followed by "a great and gloriously sticky marmalade roll."[8] I didn't understand how stickiness could be glorious (the translator gave a mostly word-by-word translation of this passage[9]), but it certainly helped that I had tasted marmalade before.

For the rest of the book, I was consumed by the story like any other reader. I found the adventure of the English children breathtaking, and I fell in love with everything about Aslan. However, there was one last moment in the book that stopped me, even though it had nothing to do with food. It was right before the climax, where Aslan appears at the Stone Table and the Witch and her evil followers surround him. Beloved Aslan is about to be put to death, in exchange for the blood of Edmund, the flan junkie.

A great crowd of people were standing all around the Stone Table.
. . . But such people! Ogres with monstrous teeth, and wolves, and
bull-headed men; spirits of evil trees and poisonous plants; and other
creatures whom I won't describe because if I did the grown-ups
would probably not let you read this book.[10]

A sudden intrusion of the omniscient narrator's voice took me out of the book. Why do I have to be reminded of "the grown-ups" at such a critical moment of the story? The use of the "God's eye view" is less common in Japanese children's books, and its condescending tone offended

---

[7]Lewis, *The Lion, the Witch and the Wardrobe*, 34.
[8]Lewis, *The Lion, the Witch and the Wardrobe*, 71.
[9]Lewis, *Raion to majo*, 106.
[10]Lewis, *The Lion, the Witch and the Wardrobe*, 148.

my ten-year-old sensibility. For me, a story would lose its magic if it smacked of any didactic intention.

Before I digress too much on the topic of my Japanese experience with Lewis, though, I'd like to make a point of returning to the other part of my lane, that of being a poet. Like most other poets who are writing poems in Japanese or English, I was trained as a lyric poet. Lyric poetry focuses on personal feelings, unlike epic or narrative poetry that tells dramatic tales. In his *Essential Poet's Glossary*, Edward Hirsch writes that the lyric "delivers on our spiritual lives precisely because it gives us the gift of intimacy and interiority, of privacy and participation."[11] This, of course, does not mean that as a lyric poet you have the license to indulge in sentimentality or personal melodramas. Any student who takes a poetry workshop in America will learn it soon enough. One of the first poetry workshops I participated in was at Harvard University. My joy of being selected for the workshop quickly faded when the instructor announced our first assignment: "Write a poem; you can do whatever you want, but please make sure that it's not about love or death or being lonely." If a poem isn't about love or death or being lonely, what else is there to talk about? I wonder to this day. Isn't Lewis's *Dymer* ostensibly about all of these things?

Perhaps it is reassuring that Lewis's poetic sensibility was kept untouched by both potential benefits and harm of such creative writing pedagogy. As Louis Menand writes in his *New Yorker* article "Show or Tell," the discipline of creative writing is an American invention. When I studied at Cambridge University, very briefly in the 1990s, I discovered that the British were mostly bemused by, if not openly contemptuous of, my desire to write my own poems in English. Tellingly, an English author and academic, Sir Malcolm Bradbury, once compared the idea of creative writing courses to "the hamburger—a vulgar hybrid which, as everyone once knew, no sensible person would ever eat."[12]

---

[11] Edward Hirsch, *Essential Poet's Glossary* (New York: Houghton Mifflin Harcourt, 2017), 169.
[12] Louis Menand, "Show or Tell," *The New Yorker*, June 8, 2009, www.newyorker.com/magazine/2009/06/08/show-or-tell.

What impresses me the most about Lewis as a poet is that he was driven by a desire to write epic poetry. This is simply unheard of in my time, but it must have been extremely rare even in the time he was writing. Three years after *Dymer* was completed, Lewis wrote a letter to his brother on August 2, 1928:

> It sounds astonishing but English poetry is one of the things that you can come to the end of, . . . that there is no longer any chance of discovering a long poem in English which will turn out to be just what I want and which can be added to the *Faerie Queen*, the *Prelude*, *Paradise Lost*, *The Ring and the Book*, the *Earthly Paradise*, and a few others—because there aren't any more. . . . In that sense I may be said to have come to the end of English poetry—as you may be said to have come to the end of a wood, not when you have actually walked every inch of it, but when you have walked about in it enough to know where all the boundaries are and to feel the end near even when you can't see it; when there is no longer any hope . . . that the next turn of the path might bring you to an unsuspected lake or cave or clearing on the edge of a new valley—when it can no longer conceal anything.[13]

Lewis's disappointment in finding no more possible space for long poems is so great that it kills his anticipation for any fresh surprise or magical encounter in what is supposed to be a vast wood of English poetry. I am tempted to argue that when one is a poet, more than a writer of any other genre, one must fight against obstacles. It could be against historical forces, the literary trends of one's own time, one's melancholic frame of mind, one's financial situation, prejudices of all kinds. I am an English-as-a-second-language writer who came to live in America in my late teens, and while my situation is completely different from Lewis's, I experienced my share of feeling unwelcome and threatened by the looming boundaries

---

[13]C. S. Lewis, *Letters of C. S. Lewis*, ed. W. H. Lewis (New York: Harcourt Brace Jovanovich, 1966), 129.

in the august forest of poetry in English. And unlike me, of course, Lewis
was gifted. Against all odds, he was convinced of his vocation to bring forth
an epic poem, "A splendour in the dark, a tale, a song,"[14] for which there
was no appreciative audience.

Concerning the mystery of one's gift, Flannery O'Connor writes that it is
"something gratuitous and wholly undeserved, something whose real uses
will probably always be hidden from us" and asserts that "the artist has to
suffer certain deprivations in order to use his gift with integrity."[15] I believe
that Lewis suffered critical deprivations as he struggled to exercise his gift as
a narrative/epic poet with integrity. His poetic gift would have no doubt
flourished were he born a few centuries earlier. Although it is impossible to
locate exact influences that shaped a single work of literature, if my task were
to look for a certain connection between *Dymer* and other narrative poetry,
I would describe *Dymer*'s characteristics as a combination of Shelley's
"Alastor" and Byron's *Don Juan*. *Dymer* is a curious amalgam of romanticism
and irony, the two forces that work hard to undermine each other's power,
and one could argue, as far as the vision behind the poem goes, it is a more
complex, sophisticated piece than either of the two poems by the major Romantic authors. It astonishes me that as a young writer Lewis could present
to the world such a lucid testament of his tortured sense of the dialectical
forces in life (romantic longing vs. irony, real vs. artificial, utopian republic
vs. anarchy) and his search for the kind of truth that transcends them, while
showcasing his mastery of poetic craft and technical fluency.

And if I were to guess what ultimately undermines the effectiveness of
Dymer, I would say that it is young Lewis's very proximity to his hero. Even
though Lewis tells Arthur Greeves that he is not Dymer,[16] it seems that he
had not established enough distance between himself and Dymer to dra-
matize and turn his character's action and thinking into a compelling story.

---

[14]Lewis, *Dymer*, V.29.

[15]Flannery O'Connor, *Mystery and Manners: Occasional Prose* (New York: Farrar, Straus and
Giroux, 1970), 81.

[16]C. S. Lewis, *The Collected Letters of C. S. Lewis*, ed. Walter Hooper, vol. 1, *Family Letters
1905–1931* (London: Harper Collins, 2000), 664.

The more earnest young Lewis is about his own search and struggles, the more Dymer ends up sounding pedantic and preachy. Dymer's prolonged journey—marked not only by physical suffering but also by a building sense of shame, self-awareness, and despair—tests the reader's patience by its relentless monotony.

I agree with Dr. Root that in *Dymer* there are a number of things in germ that will blossom into full flower in Lewis's later projects. The way Dr. Root painstakingly traces a literary DNA of Lewis's prose in *Dymer* is impressive. However, because there are so many moments in *Dymer* that can be connected to so many later works by Lewis, I find the number of examples overwhelming, and I am afraid that it's easy to lose sight of what the point of it all was to begin with. To simply prove the interconnectedness in all the books Lewis wrote by following the development of each motif or idea could be a tedious task.

In fact, I would be more interested in hearing about how Lewis's primary sense of himself as a poet affected his later prose works. It is the case with most writers that their early ideas end up becoming fully developed in their later projects. However, for Lewis, that had to happen in a genre that is the opposite of poetry. As a gifted, ambitious poet, he had to go through a kind of dying-to-self process. What sacrifices did Lewis make and what inventions was he able to accomplish as he went back and forth between the two literary modes, whose priorities and economy are often vastly different?

Once awake from his dream, Dymer bitterly recounts his imaginary meeting with his beloved woman to the magician:

> "So beautiful, she seemed
> Almost a living soul. But every part
> Was what I made it—all that I had dreamed—
> No more, no less: the mirror of my heart,
> Such things as boyhood feigns beneath the smart
> Of solitude and spring."[17]

---

[17]Lewis, *Dymer*, VII.20.

Instead of "the very core of truth" that is "beyond all veils,"[18] what Dymer ends up embracing is himself. This is a critical moment; though not for the first time, Lewis's hero clearly and painfully recognizes magic as ultimately a solipsistic enterprise. In the later scene, Dymer accuses the same goddess-like woman of deluding him, and she gives a haunting answer: "For our kind must come to all / If bidden, but in the shape for which they call."[19]

As Dr. Root points out, Lewis's notion that "reality is iconoclastic" is distinctly present in *Dymer*. This search for what is really real is no doubt one of the ideas that become developed in full blossom in Lewis's prose. What Lewis's hero fails to seize, "the very core of truth," exerts such power that any lesser reality or fantastical vision born of self-centered desires must be rendered lifeless. I believe that truth is the ultimate magic, which establishes a clear hierarchy in Lewis's world. And perhaps it explains the didacticism I sensed in his writing as a ten-year-old girl.

The goddess figure, who identifies herself as "the loved one, the long lost," makes a symbolic remark to Dymer: "You should have asked my name."[20] Indeed, on several different occasions, Lewis's poem reminds the reader of the fact that her name is unknown to Dymer. In a way, Lewis's later works continue to ask her name, her face, the ultimate destination for an endless longing which always points beyond, what Lewis called "*Sehnsucht*," where poetry and reality are not at odds against each other.

---

[18]Lewis, *Dymer*, VII.24.
[19]Lewis, *Dymer*, VIII.13.
[20]Lewis, *Dymer*, VIII.6.

CONTRIBUTORS

Jeffry C. Davis (PhD, University of Illinois at Chicago) is professor of English and dean of humanities at Wheaton College, where he directs the nationally recognized interdisciplinary studies program. He is the author of *Interdisciplinary Inclinations: Reflections for Students Integrating Liberal Arts and Christian Faith.*

David C. Downing (PhD, University of California at Los Angeles) is the codirector of the Marion E. Wade Center at Wheaton College. Downing is the author of four books on C. S. Lewis, as well as a novel, *Looking for the King.* Downing is also an editor and annotator of the *Wade Annotated Pilgrim's Regress* and *C. S. Lewis's Letters on Faith* (forthcoming).

Mark Lewis (MFA, Southern Methodist University) is a professor and the director of theater at Wheaton College, where he has taught and led the theater ensemble, *Workout,* for twenty-five years. He has directed almost fifty plays in that time at Wheaton, in New York, and for Wheaton's *Shakespeare in the Park.*

Miho Nonaka (PhD, University of Houston) is associate professor of English at Wheaton College, where she teaches literature and creative writing. She is the author of *The Museum of Small Bones.* Her poems and essays have appeared in various journals and anthologies, including *Missouri Review, Southern Review, Kenyon Review, Ploughshares, American Letters & Commentary, Iowa Review, Tin House,* and *American Odysseys: Writings by New American.*

Jerry Root (PhD, Open University) is professor of evangelism and leadership at Wheaton College and visiting professor at Biola University and Moody Bible Institute. He has authored or coauthored nine books (seven on C. S. Lewis) and lectured about Lewis at eighty universities in nineteen countries. He is also a member of the Wade Center advisory board and serves as the Christopher W. Mitchell Senior Fellow for C. S. Lewis Studies of the C. S. Lewis Institute.

INDEX TO *DYMER:*
WADE ANNOTATED EDITION

AUTHOR INDEX

SUBJECT INDEX

The Marion E. Wade Center

Founded in 1965, the Marion E. Wade Center of Wheaton College, Illinois, houses a major research collection of writings and related materials by and about seven British authors: Owen Barfield, G. K. Chesterton, C. S. Lewis, George MacDonald, Dorothy L. Sayers, J. R. R. Tolkien, and Charles Williams. The Wade Center collects, preserves, and makes these resources available to researchers and visitors through its reading room, museum displays, educational programming, and publications. All of these endeavors are a tribute to the importance of the literary, historical, and Christian heritage of these writers. Together, these seven authors form a school of thought, as they valued and promoted the life of the mind and the imagination. Through service to those who use its resources and by making known the words of its seven authors, the Wade Center strives to continue their legacy.

THE HANSEN LECTURESHIP SERIES

The Ken and Jean Hansen Lectureship is an annual lecture series named in honor of former Wheaton College trustee Ken Hansen and his wife, Jean, and endowed in their memory by Walter and Darlene Hansen. The series features three lectures per academic year by a Wheaton College faculty member on one or more of the Wade Center authors with responses by fellow faculty members.

Kenneth and Jean (née Hermann) Hansen are remembered for their welcoming home, deep appreciation for the imagination and the writings of the Wade authors, a commitment to serving others, and their strong Christian faith. After graduation from Wheaton College, Ken began working with Marion Wade in his residential cleaning business (later renamed ServiceMaster) in 1947. After Marion's death in 1973, Ken Hansen was instrumental in establishing the Marion E. Wade Collection at Wheaton College in honor of his friend and business colleague.